JOHN HANSON OF MULBERRY GROVE

JOHN HANSON
From Portrait by Charles Willson Peale in Independence Hall

JOHN HANSON
of Mulberry Grove

By

J. BRUCE KREMER

ALBERT & CHARLES BONI, INC.
NEW YORK
1938

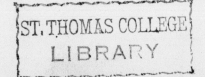

PRINTED IN THE UNITED STATES OF AMERICA
BY THE CORNWALL PRESS, INC., CORNWALL, N. Y.

To Cornelia

PREFACE

$\mathcal{N}$O PEOPLE TAKE GREATER
pride and pleasure in the study of our history than
we of the Free State of Maryland. Many of our
able students and brilliant writers have furnished
us with hours of deep satisfaction by laying before
us the stories of an honored past. A respect for
the freedom which was won by blood and tears is
an essential in the character of our commonwealth. The results of every new work of research
and study of the pioneering days when a wilderness was being changed into a land of happiness
and plenty are read throughout our state with
gratified attention.

I have always taken a Marylander's pleasure in
this subject of our land, its development through
earliest colonial struggle and adventure to the
virile, fighting democracy of the Revolution, and
thereafter as a virile, fighting democracy remaining worthy of its title as the Free State. Few
manuscripts dealing with that history have given

me more pleasure than the work of Mr. Kremer, including its tracing of the injection of the Scandinavian blood stream into the earliest life of the Maryland colony, and to observing some of its results in the history of our people.

Mr. Kremer gratifies all of us who cherish and respect the memory of men capable of standing for the right, steadfast in the face of major opposition, with the vivid story of "John Hanson of Mulberry Grove." I have no recollection of seeing the history of this great patriot of Maryland so carefully compiled, nor so adequately set forth in a background of his ancestry, his surroundings, his problems and his service. That he was given the highest federal honor ever accorded to a man of Maryland, the Presidency of the Continental Congress, is known to most of us. By what magnificent and constant effort in the great struggle for independence he more than earned such honors, is excellently told to us by Mr. Kremer.

I am told that J. Bruce Kremer is not of Scandinavian ancestry, and that his tribute to the sometimes neglected glory of the Swedish and Finnish pioneers in Delaware and Maryland is that of the student and historian, rather than of the compatriot and partisan. Indeed it should be recorded that Mr. Kremer made these studies and wrote

PREFACE

this volume from even more unselfish motives
than are suggested by his modest introduction. As
a citizen of Maryland, proud of every chapter of
her history and eager that each should be more
adequately told, I express to the author, for his
work, my most sincere gratitude.

HARRY W. NICE,
Governor of Maryland.

INTRODUCTION

𝒯HE YEAR 1938 IS THE
occasion of numerous official commemorations of
the first landing of the Swedes and Finns on the
Delaware River three hundred years earlier, in
1638. During the three centuries between the
event itself and today there has been a great deal
of history written about the foundation of America, and a great deal of omission from such history
respecting the establishment of New Sweden and
the initial introduction of the Scandinavian blood
stream into the life of the new world. Many an
American school child is quite as confident that
William Penn was the first settler in Pennsylvania,
as that the Puritans settled New England. That
Pennsylvania and Delaware were New Sweden for
a number of years before Penn received his charter, and that the Scandinavians pioneered on the
North American continent as surely as did the
English and the Dutch, is of itself a fact in history
which needs telling to our American people.

The Delaware Valley Tercentenary Celebration
of 1938 and the courtesy of the Governor of Maryland in appointing me to the chairmanship of
Maryland's Tercentenary Commission might be
considered adequate reasons for the compilation
of this volume. The fact that the property of Mulberry Grove, in Charles County, Maryland, which
had been the birthplace and home of John Hanson, came into my possession some years ago, is a
more personal reason for preserving in print those
facts which have been available about the great
statesman whose grandfather came to New Sweden
in 1642 and to Maryland shortly thereafter, leaving a long and potent line of children, grandchildren and collateral kin, to play their heroic parts
on the stage of American life.

It is my hope and intention to restore the manor
house as near as possible to its original form, thus
to preserve one more of our important colonial
landmarks.

One further motivating influence upon the author arose through a good many years of residence
and activity in the Northwest, and especially in
the state of Montana, where I was thrown inti-
mately into contact with the Scandinavian pioneers of the more recent decades and had abundant opportunity through their daily friendship

to acquire deep respect for the courage and independence of their character, the soundness of their faith in democratic ideals of civilized social order, and the tremendous capacity of the whole of the Scandinavian races to build farms and homes and cities in a new land.

There is a long gap in years between the first settlement of the Swedes and Finns on the shores of the Delaware in the seventeenth century, and the settlement of the Swedes and Danes, Finns and Norwegians, in the great areas ranging chiefly from Michigan westward to Puget Sound and onward into Alaska in the nineteenth and twentieth centuries. There is no gap at all between the strength and vigor of the pioneers in Delaware, Pennsylvania, Maryland and New Jersey who built the first log cabins in America three hundred years ago, and that of the pioneers of Michigan, Wisconsin and Minnesota, of the Dakotas, Montana, Idaho and Washington, who hewed the timber of the north woods and broke the ground of the far prairies. Of these latter pioneers it has been my privilege to know many, and to call them friends. My best tribute to their contribution to American life is to perpetuate herein, so far as I am able, the story of the pioneering of their countrymen in earlier times, and their role in the foundation of a white man's world in North America, and the particular contribution of John Hanson of Mulberry Grove to the creation of a free and independent nation, a perpetual union of American colonies to form the United States of America.

This account of the pioneers of New Sweden and their descendants in Maryland, and of the statesmanship of one of them in particular, is offered with no claims to scholarship or literary merit. I wish that both were greater. I would think the book worth offering even if they were less. The substance is worth perpetuating, regardless of the form. Leaning in many details upon the research of better students and finer writers, I may state only that it has been my purpose to present authenticated facts in a background of the time and circumstance in which they occurred.

There is no occasion for undue amplification of what the founders of New Sweden contributed to the making of this country, or of what Hanson contributed to the formation of this nation. There is much occasion to perpetuate in memory and in the record of our history the very definite accomplishment of those people and of that man. It has not been my intention to make comparisons or take part in controversies. Each step in history was preceded and followed by other steps. To select a single one and to insist that but for the doing of that very thing, all other things would have been left undone and all other accomplishments of no avail, appears to me only a warped use of the advantages of hind sight. History is a pattern of many parts, and in placing before the public a record of one part, the author must restrain his natural enthusiasm for his task and his momentary conclusion that this part excelleth and exceeds all others.

With a considered opinion that the parts of our American history included in this modest volume have not received adequate attention among the many parts of the whole pattern, and in the hope that they are here set forth in sufficient adequacy to commend the interest of a respectable number of understanding readers, the work is offered to the American public.

J. B. K.

May, 1938.

CONTENTS

CONTENTS

ILLUSTRATIONS

19

ILLUSTRATIONS

Chapter 1

SWEDISH COLONIES ON THE DELAWARE

$\mathcal{I}$N THE MIDDLE OF MARCH
in the year 1638 two small vessels which since the
end of the previous December had been buffeted
by the storms of the North Atlantic made a safe
harbor in Delaware Bay and under favorable
wind and tide proceeded up the river of that
name to the mouth of the Minquas Kill, a small
stream which was to have many names before it
should be known as the Brandywine. The ship
Kalmar Nyckel and the yacht *Fogel Grip* each
flew the flag of Sweden. They were commanded
by a Dutchman named Peter Minuit, were
manned by Swedish and Dutch sailors and carried
enough Swedish soldiers to form a small garrison.
They brought a handful of emigrants from Sweden and from Finland, the latter country having
then been long a part of Sweden. The cargoes
included foods and material supplies for the proposed settlement, but chiefly cloth and axes and

23

knives and other articles suitable for trading with the Indians.

For about two English miles the little ships sailed up the Minquas Kill, making their landing at a "bridge of stones" or natural wharf suitable for debarkation. Then and there was founded the first Scandinavian colony in the New World, now the city of Wilmington, Delaware.

The log of the voyage to America was lost, possibly when Peter Minuit disappeared from history a few months later in a hurricane off the island of St. Christopher. Sufficient records of the many Atlantic crossings of the period are available to leave no reasonable question that the crew, soldiers and settlers on the "Key of Colmar" and the "Bird Griffin," as they would be called in English, were very tired men and women, and many of them very ill. Some unquestionably died in the crossing. Such ailments as scurvy were so commonly a feature of the passage of the great ocean as to be the rule rather than the exception. Food supplies were limited, and for the most part execrable. Water frequently ran short. Bathing on shipboard probably was not thought of. No physicians tended on the sick, but homely remedies familiar to the seasoned mariners may have been administered by the ships' masters. Crowding was the common practice. Accidents were numerous. Sailors and passengers alike might be lost overboard in storms.

The passage of the first Swedish colonists was not of long duration in comparison with other voyages of the time, for six months was no more unusual than three. Many navigators shunned the northern routes and crossed from northern Europe via Portugal, the Canary Islands, and the West Indies, where weather was considered more propitious and harbors for shelter, supplies, water, and repairs more numerous and better known. The cumbersome shallow vessels, square rigged, had little capacity for tacking against the wind, and lay often for weeks in harbor waiting for the winds to shift. Minuit indeed had planned his course from Gothenburg through the North Sea and to the north of Scotland and had put out once in November, 1637, only to be buffeted about for a month in hostile gales and then forced into Texel sorely battered, the *Kalmar Nyckel* without prow or main mast, the *Fogel Grip* leaking, the poor adventurers physically sore beset and needing the added weeks of respite while repairs were made, new victuals and fresh water put aboard. There is no record that any of them withdrew, but rather that six new emigrants had joined the party. The men of the north country looked in the face of nature at her worst, and were unafraid. It is not strange that when a landing had been made upon the Delaware they lost no moment in offering profound thanks to Almighty God for all his mercy in their behalf. He had brought them to their destination, weary and battered, it is true, but safe. They had their lives, and most of their cargoes, and the spring sunshine fell over the wooded slopes along the river where the first buds were on the trees. Friendly natives, watching the progress of their vessels up the river, came to make them welcome. The Indians knew something already of the advantage of trading with the white men.

For only eighteen years would the new colony live under the flag of Sweden, then for a brief eight years as part of Dutch New Amsterdam, and thenceforward under British rule more than a century until the day of Independence. Throughout this period, however, it was destined to retain much of its Scandinavian character and racial basis, and from it were to go out large numbers of the simple, stalwart men and women into the settlements of Pennsylvania, New Jersey and Maryland. Of the pioneers to the latter state was to be a certain John Hanson, who would give to his new land many sons, and grandsons, and great grandsons. And one of those would sign himself "President of the United States in Congress Assembled."

The founding of the first Scandinavian colony on the Delaware, and the ten subsequent expeditions which added to the numbers of the settlers in the two decades after 1638, found their motives in a mixture of commercial enterprise and patriotic aspiration in the fatherland. Sweden in the opening years of the 17th century was rising to the summit of her power as the dominant force in northern Europe. No more vigorous, alert, courageous and adventurous nation then existed. Beginning two generations earlier under the great Vasa, the Swedes had come into a period of military triumph and industrial awakening. Under Gustavus Adolphus they completed their victories over Russia and Poland and strode rapidly onward toward that virile monarch's vision of the Baltic as a Swedish Lake. Denmark, perched at the essential outlet, was in turn brought to account, and the balance of Protestant Europe turned to the great Swedish leader as their chief and saviour in the Thirty Years War. The English and Dutch, whether united or at swords points, each cultivated the friendship of the northern power.

With military victory grew the opportunities of trade, and with improved domestic order under the wisdom of the great Gustavus grew industrial advancement in such enterprises as steel and iron making, copper mining, and allied trades. Swedish cannon were the pride of every nation which could buy them, and Swedish swords acquired a distinction not hitherto enjoyed by any but Damascus blades. The Dutch, having first freed their merchants and their workmen from the feudal yoke, became the trading nation, sending their ships around the world, forming the first great corporations and trusts, their Dutch East Indies Company and their Dutch West Indies Company. For years two-thirds of the expanding trade of the Baltic went in bottoms owned in the States General of the Netherlands. Another portion went in vessels of the equally aspiring English. And then Sweden turned more of her energy to ship building and began to cast her eyes beyond the seven seas, and to wonder why she need import her spices from the Indies and her tobacco from America through the barriers of Dutch customs. In the same fashion the advantages of exports in iron, copper and other goods

28

by Swedish ships became apparent, with visions of the Swedish skippers hunting out new markets as they cruised the seven seas.

Gustavus Adolphus fell at Lützen in 1632. His death delayed, but did not destroy, his dream of commerce toward the far horizons. He had given brief attention to the plans of Dutch and Swedish capitalists for the formation of the South Company, a venture variously aimed at commerce in North America, Guinea, and Africa. The limitations of capital in the Swedish countries, outside of the royal funds, caused any venture at that period to await the seal of royalty. The emancipated Dutch already had arrived at a condition where the rich merchants controlled the government, and armies and navies protected the trading of the great commercial groups. In Sweden the concentrated wealth remained largely with the king and his nobility, but the virus of commercial progress had begun to do its work, wealthy freemen were becoming numerous in Stockholm and Gothenburg, and the nobility had learned to seek for opportunities of revenue outside the rents or taxes of their lands and forests.

Christina, the daughter of Gustavus, was a minor child. The state council of leading men took over the reins of government. Count Axel Oxen-

stierna, the royal chancellor, began to put together
the remaining parts of plans half nurtured before
the tragedy of Lützen, and to develop them ex-
tensively. Out of the old South company came
the New Sweden Company, again partially fi-
nanced and inspired by the Dutch. Into it the
chancellor put substantial contributions of his
own wealth, and he induced other Swedish noble-
men to buy its shares. As in the scheme envi-
sioned by Gustavus, it was in part an enterprise
for profit, and part a project for the settlement of
Scandinavians over seas so that their flag might
fly over new and large domains, rivalling the
banners of the British and the Dutch.

England had found her first place in the new
World in Virginia soon after the beginning of the
century, and later the settlements in New England had been founded by the Pilgrims. Lord
Baltimore had opened the colony of Maryland in
1634. The Dutch had sent out Henry Hudson to
find the westward passage to the Indies, and New
Amsterdam had been settled in 1614. The French
had taken permanent foot in Canada in 1608.
Spain had of course preceded all of them in col-
onization to the south. To none of these, nor to
the fiery Poles nor the fierce Cossacks, did Sweden
bow on land. Had she not every right and title

to assume her portion of the spoils across the sea? Long before Columbus, the Norsemen had been the white discoverers of America.

Religious freedom was not a dominating problem in the Scandinavian world. Early converted to Lutheranism, the northern peoples had shown much early and firm leaning toward tolerance of all Christian worship. A potent strain of individualism runs in Swedish veins. A people loving liberty, and given to respect for it. Their trek to new lands along the Delaware was not, therefore, a religious pilgrimage. Religion had come with the settlers but religious questions had not sent them to America. Patriotism and profit sponsored the colony.

The lure of gold and silver, long dominant as a magnet to draw adventurers to America, was also largely missing from the Swedish calculations. Peter Minuit, when he set out with the *Kalmar Nyckel* and the *Fogel Grip,* knew of his own experience that precious metals in large areas of North America were at best an unknown quantity. He had already served the Dutch company at New Amsterdam. Precious furs, most notably the beaver, he knew abounded. Tobacco was being raised and could be raised. Iron ore had been discovered in abundance, but the natives of the north had meagre ornaments of gold. The British and the Dutch had long since found privateering on the Spanish treasure ships the most profitable form of mining in the western world. At the end of the Thirty Years War such operations gradually fell into disfavor, and there is at least some moderation in the limited record of such piracy promoted by the Swedes. One of their expeditions to the new world actually suffered frightfully at Spanish hands, but most of them received favorable treatment when they called for water or supplies in the West Indies, and there was some trading by Swedish ships in those localities.

When Minuit landed at Minquas Kill in 1638, his first business was negotiations with the Indians for the purchase of their lands. At a conference with five chiefs, or sachems, the transaction was accomplished with apparent promptness. Historians have never located the exact deeds executed at that time, but records of subsequent arrangements in which those deeds are quoted indicate that Minuit purchased lands northward from Minquas Kill (Wilmington) to the mouth of the Schuylkill, just south of modern Philadelphia, and to the southward from Minquas Kill about 40 miles. The purchased land extended

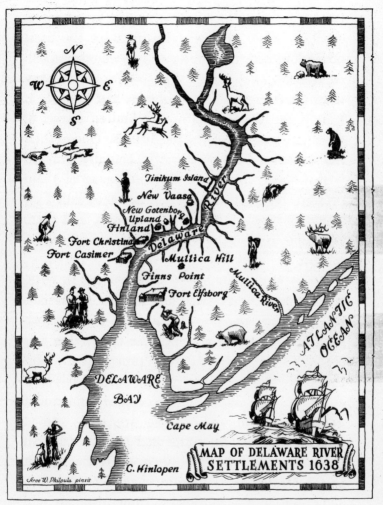

Tinikum Island

New Vaasa

New Gotenborg
Upland
Finland

Fort Christina

Fort Casimer

Delaware River

Mullica Hill

Finns Point

Fort Elfsborg

Mullica River

ATLANTIC OCEAN

DELAWARE BAY

Cape May

C. Hinlopen

Arne W. Philpula pinxit

MAP OF DELAWARE RIVER
SETTLEMENTS 1638

westward for an undefined and therefore indefi-
nite distance. Most often the white purchasers
of those days assumed that their right went westward to the Pacific Ocean, if indeed they had any
knowledge about that body of water. Its distance
from the Atlantic was an entirely unknown quantity. It is difficult, to say the least, to determine
at this time what was in the minds of the Indian
grantors. Probably it was difficult then. That
the redskins were not without guile in their transactions appears reasonably evident, although some
of their repeated sales of the same territory to a
variety of ambitious white men may have resulted
from ignorance of language and writing, and inad-
equacy of interpretation. One might be excused
for confusion in drafting a deed by the sign language. Quite possibly the natives had no very
precise idea about land ownership in the Cauca-
sian sense, and were disposing from time to time
of what they regarded as a more or less temporary
right to hunt, fish, trap or trade furs over a given
area. The Europeans undoubtedly adopted the
views most favorable to their own interest, and
once a group of Indian sachems had made their
marks upon a paper, and walked off with a supply
of trading goods, the purchasers drew their own

maps and laid the ground work for their subsequent interpretations of the claims.

Whatever the attendant circumstances, the first purchase by Minuit unquestionably covered considerable areas already claimed with much semblance of authority by Lord Baltimore under the charter of Maryland, and others subsequently to be given by British royal grant to William Penn. The Dutch had likewise made purchases in some of the area described, and on the basis of "indefinitely westward," might have laid claim to all of it. Many years later the famous Mason and Dixon's line was run straight across the middle of the region. Nevertheless the area was unsettled by other white men when it was taken by the Crown of Sweden, and that claim, being backed by settlement and occupation of some small portion of the area, was as good, and perhaps better, than any which previously or subsequently was contested. The same may as well be said regarding many subsequent acquisitions by the Swedish settlers, whose complete territorial assertions during the period of Swedish sovereignty in the New World extended along both shores of the Delaware from Cape May and Cape Henlopen to points well northward of the Schuylkill, ranging westward in the usual fashion of terrestrial perpetuity, and eastward into the Jerseys to an undefined contact point with the Dutch claims from New Amsterdam.

The uncertainties arising through the claims of discovery and the purchases from the natives beset the settlers in all parts of North America for many years. With exploration, trading rivalry, and settlement, the meaning of boundaries became realistic. Old deeds were examined with new care. In the case of New Sweden, long after the Swedish rights were obliterated by conquest, historians sought to determine with certainty whether or not Charles I of England had ceded to Sweden the discovery rights claimed by the British on the Delaware. That academic question remains disputed. The practical problem was settled by the Dutch and then the British by force of arms. In the intervening years a number of boundary disputes existed, and subsequent to the British control there were continuing discussions of the Maryland line. A glance at any modern map will demonstrate how little the early settlers knew of the geography of their new land, or the extent of other grants. Even the first purchase by Peter Minuit from the five sachems on the Delaware was assumed to include areas to the westward covering the larger part of what is now the

state of Maryland. It seems certain that Minuit
knew of Lord Baltimore's settlement, but equally
certain that he had very vague notions of the
geography of Chesapeake Bay or the land beyond
it, and was unaware that lands and waters of the
Maryland grant lay but a few miles to the westward of his landing place.

It was to be some years after the landing of the
Kalmar and the *Grip* before any contact would be
had with settlers to the west and southwest, but
next to no time at all before the problem of the
Dutch settlers would be met. The Dutch had
been among the first explorers on the river, and
they had been both the most frequent and most
recent visitors. They believed that Henry Hudson's earliest voyage antedated the English in
Virginia, who knew of the large bay to the northward, and called it "de la Ware" after their
governor. About 1616, a Dutch skipper named
Hendricksen had made mention of the bay and
river. A few years later Cornelius Mey, or May,
visited the river and gave his name to the cape at
its eastern entrance.

Then about 1623 May came back and built the
first Dutch settlement, or trading post, called Fort
Nassau and located not far from the present site
of Gloucester, New Jersey, on the eastern bank.

This post probably was not continuously occupied, but a small garrison was there when Minuit came. In the meantime a small settlement had been attempted on the west bank, farther downstream, but had been wiped out by the Indians. The Dutch West India Company certainly thought of the Delaware, or South River, as they called it in distinction from the North River, or Hudson, as its own. It probably had made purchases of land from the Indians at some points along the stream. The Swedish pioneers found a Captain May, possibly the earlier explorer, commanding at Fort Nassau and firmly asserting that the Hollanders possessed the entire river. Minuit probably asserted just as much in behalf of Queen Christina, and no immediate difficulties ensued when the Swedes built their Fort Christina at Minquas Kill and made no moves toward trading on the upper river.

The history of the Swedish settlements upon the Delaware has been told frequently, and well. Their own pastors, notably Campanius and Acrelius, recorded it. In the United States the comprehensive works of Dr. Amandus Johnson, backed by his research in the libraries of Stockholm, has given us in one text a comprehensive story.

Each of the expeditions which followed one another from the homeland was in itself a brave adventure, and each added to the sturdy little group of colonists. The large expedition which brought Governor Johan Printz in 1643 as commander of the colony brought also four brothers of the family Hanson, whom we will meet again in Maryland a few years later. Under Printz new forts were built and cultivation of the land progressed as vigorously as trading with the natives. Settlements opened on the east bank of the river. Adventurers went far afield into the interior, searching for minerals as well as pelts. Minor conflicts with the Dutch arose, as well as trading with New Amsterdam, and there were trading visits from the settlers of Virginia to the south, and New England to the north.

Now and then contact was made overland with the English pioneers in Maryland, although the trails, if any permanent ones could be said to exist, were wild and rugged. Occasionally a Scandinavian colonist, tempted by visions of richer fields farther from home, moved off to settle in Maryland, or even in Virginia. A few were wooed over to New Amsterdam, to take citizenship among the Dutch. After the Dutch conquest of New Sweden, a bloodless expedition under Peter Stuyvesant in

1656, migration by the Scandivanian settlers became more common. Those who remained took oaths of allegiance to the States General, and within a decade changed their allegiance again, perforce, to British. Dutch or British as need be by force of sovereignty, they remained Swedes and Finns by instinct and, for years, by language. For a century after their loss as colonists of the Swedish crown, the Swedish Church sent pastors over to them, and supplied them Bibles and other reading matter. Even between the Swedes and Finns, because of difference in language, there long remained some group distinctions, chiefly through the establishment of churches using the Finnish tongue. One settlement at what is now Chester, Pennsylvania, for some years had the name of Finland.

The total of Scandinavian colonists coming from the old world to New Sweden in the two decades after 1638 is not absolutely established. It is probable that their number did not exceed one thousand. Certainly no more than that number were living in the settlements along the Delaware for any large part of that period. These few, their children and their children's children made upon the New World an impress disproportionate to their numbers. Although ultimately conquered by the Dutch who by sheer overwhelming force of numbers swallowed their little settlements one by one, they had long and firmly resisted the assertions of their neighbors, and kept their colony intact for years when almost any show of armed force could have subdued them.

One faculty contributing greatly to their success was that of friendly understandings with the natives. They traded much and fought little with the Indians, and it is not unfair to say that this performance rested on a high degree of honesty in native dealings. Records are abundant showing that many tribes of redskins were their friends, preferred to deal with them, and warned them of their enemies. The men of New Sweden ventured far afield with Indian companions, hunting, trading and exploring. One menace of the wilderness about them, the menace of the tomahawk, harassed them less than was the case with other white men. Evidently they paid well in their transactions, for Dutch and English records tell of "underselling" by the Swedes "ruining the trade."

They worked hard and to effect. Cattle, sheep and swine they brought to America and bred, and horses when they could afford them. Independent men of spirit in the manner of their northern homeland, they protested and resisted too much

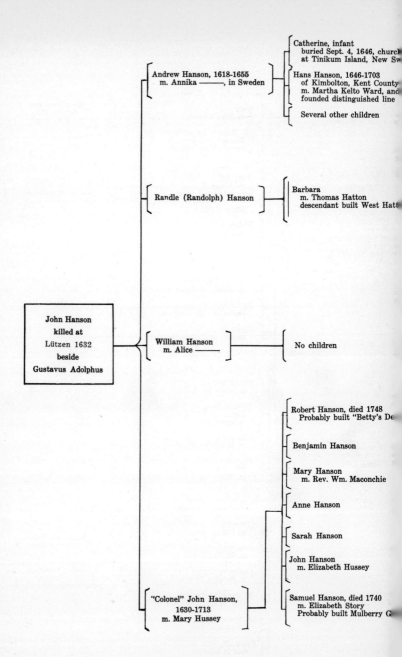

John Hanson
killed at
Lützen 1632
beside
Gustavus Adolphus

Andrew Hanson, 1618-1655
m. Annika ———, in Sweden

Catherine, infant
buried Sept. 4, 1646, churc
at Tinikum Island, New Sw

Hans Hanson, 1646-1703
of Kimbolton, Kent County
m. Martha Kelto Ward, and
founded distinguished line

Several other children

Randle (Randolph) Hanson

Barbara
m. Thomas Hatton
descendant built West Hatt

William Hanson
m. Alice ———

No children

"Colonel" John Hanson,
1630-1713
m. Mary Hussey

Robert Hanson, died 1748
Probably built "Betty's De

Benjamin Hanson

Mary Hanson
m. Rev. Wm. Maconchie

Anne Hanson

Sarah Hanson

John Hanson
m. Elizabeth Hussey

Samuel Hanson, died 1740
m. Elizabeth Story
Probably built Mulberry G

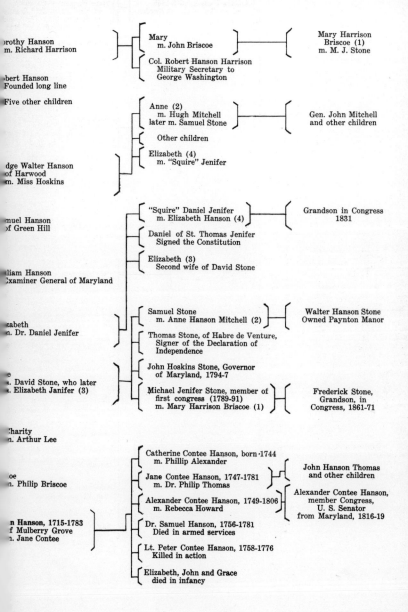

orothy Hanson
m. Richard Harrison

bert Hanson
Founded long line

Five other children

dge Walter Hanson
of Harwood
m. Miss Hoskins

muel Hanson
of Green Hill

liam Hanson
xaminer General of Maryland

zabeth
n. Dr. Daniel Jenifer

e
. David Stone, who later
. Elizabeth Janifer (3)

harity
n. Arthur Lee

oe
n. Philip Briscoe

n Hanson, 1715-1783
f Mulberry Grove
n. Jane Contee

Mary
m. John Briscoe

Col. Robert Hanson Harrison
Military Secretary to
George Washington

Mary Harrison
Briscoe (1)
m. M. J. Stone

Anne (2)
m. Hugh Mitchell
later m. Samuel Stone

Other children

Elizabeth (4)
m. "Squire" Jenifer

Gen. John Mitchell
and other children

"Squire" Daniel Jenifer
m. Elizabeth Hanson (4)

Daniel of St. Thomas Jenifer
Signed the Constitution

Elizabeth (3)
Second wife of David Stone

Grandson in Congress
1831

Samuel Stone
m. Anne Hanson Mitchell (2)

Thomas Stone, of Habre de Venture,
Signer of the Declaration of
Independence

John Hoskins Stone, Governor
of Maryland, 1794-7

Michael Jenifer Stone, member of
first congress (1789-91)
m. Mary Harrison Briscoe (1)

Walter Hanson Stone
Owned Paynton Manor

Frederick Stone,
Grandson, in
Congress, 1861-71

Catherine Contee Hanson, born 1744
m. Phillip Alexander

Jane Contee Hanson, 1747-1781
m. Dr. Philip Thomas

Alexander Contee Hanson, 1749-1806
m. Rebecca Howard

Dr. Samuel Hanson, 1756-1781
Died in armed services

Lt. Peter Contee Hanson, 1758-1776
Killed in action

Elizabeth, John and Grace
died in infancy

John Hanson Thomas
and other children

Alexander Contee Hanson,
member Congress,
U. S. Senator
from Maryland, 1816-19

governing by their own administrators, and thereafter by those of Holland and of England. After
their territory was granted finally to William Penn
they maintained with stubbornness a measure of
home rule in the "three southern counties," and
found their nearest English and Dutch neighbors
ultimately sharing with them a distaste for government from Philadelphia. From this feeling
Delaware developed as a separate state.

The assertions of their rights were usually
quiet and determined, unaccompanied by swash-
buckling or bloodshed. When Stuyvesant in New
Amsterdam took over the management of their
colony, various rules were issued to his viceroys
for the government of the Swedes. At times they
would be ordered to move into certain towns, the
better to be observed by local garrisons. Frequently they simply did not move. The Dutch
garrisons were small and hesitated to act against
them. Left to their own devices they were industrious, home loving, peaceful citizens. The rulers
who were set over them usually found it was easier
and cheaper to accept them as they were. If they
longed for a restoration of Swedish sovereignty,
and perhaps prayed for the appearance of an expedition from the Baltic, they did not bother

greatly with conspiracy or intrigue. There was, indeed, too much work to be done.

So they lived through the generations before the American revolution, changing gradually to the common language of the colonies, adopting easily the common customs, contributing to the growing wealth and raising sons and daughters for the growing population. When the great and fearful day arrived when men should stand on the side of freedom or of submission, the descendants of the Swedes along the Delaware, wherever scattered through the colonies, were found aligned for independence. One of them was to send out from Maryland the first armed force to march over Mason and Dixon's line and on into New England, to take its place beside the Green Mountain and White Mountain boys under the banner of George Washington.

Chapter II

THE SWEDES IN COLONIAL MARYLAND

$\mathcal{T}$HOSE WHO TRAVEL BY motor road from Wilmington or Newcastle in Delaware toward points in Maryland are following a route not greatly distant from the earliest Indian trail across the lands that separate the Chesapeake waters from the Delaware. The first Swedish settlers at Fort Christina (Wilmington) and Fort Casimir (Newcastle) soon found their way westward up Christina Creek and over to the headwaters of the Elk River, flowing toward the Chesapeake. The speeding motorist today covers that journey in less than an hour. In early years the huntsman, trapper, or trader would have gone by land no farther than present Elkton, for men did not plod toilsomely through forest trails when waterways opened the path for swift canoes. Those first explorers moved warily, and probably with friendly Minquas guides, for the strong and fierce Susquehannas claimed dominion of the upper

45

Chesapeake, and could not always be relied upon as friendly.

Maryland is recorded in some histories as being first settled by the expedition under Calvert in 1634, and Delaware as first settled by the Swedish expedition of 1638. That William Claiborne from Virginia may have settled on Kent Island about 1631, and the Dutch may have built and lost a settlement on the Delaware at the same period are matters of consequence only because they may have been proximate causes for later deeds. The heirs to all the claims arising from exploration, settlement, purchase from Indians and grants from European powers were destined to meet, quarrel, fight, fraternize, marry and breed strong sons and grandsons and great grandsons who would fight together for the making of a new nation. Before that union could be born there must be years of slow, hard won progress, frought with boundary disputes, religious wars, Indian wars, reflexes from European wars, trade wars, and the steady war of man against the elements in a new land. Such a land, above all else, had need for men. Some of those who would mold the future of Maryland came out of Scandinavia to the Delaware, and over the trail to Elk River. Their number was not great, their means but the strength of body and the courage which had brought them so far. They adopted so readily the ways of the Englishman already in the colony that they formed no separate groups, but spread rapidly here and there among the settlements. They married among their new neighbors and became one with them. On the shores of the Chesapeake and the Potomac the melting pot of European immigration found one of its earliest expressions.

They came from a land generally underpopulated, in which the pressure of government had rested more or less lightly upon the individual, and their instinct for freedom from restraint was strong. They wanted land, knew how to cultivate it, and disliked taxes as heartily as most common folks. In the century and a third before the American Revolution the Scandinavian pioneers and their descendants were generally aligned with the forces resentful of intrusions of the trans-Atlantic powers. When the final test came it would be the grandson of a youth who trekked over the Elk River trail who would share with the descendant of a pioneer from England the first honors in Maryland's firm stand for liberty. The statues of John Hanson and Charles Carroll today represent Maryland in Statuary Hall in the Capitol at Washington.

It is doubtful whether research can ascertain precisely which Scandinavian settlers came first from Delaware to Maryland. Of the group who landed at Minquas Kill in 1638 it is unlikely that any migrated far for several years. The colony received its first substantial growth in numbers with the coming of Governor Printz in 1643, and from that time onward tended to spread out geographically. Any efforts of the adventurous or dissatisfied to leave the colony, either for New Amsterdam, New England or Maryland, were rigidly discouraged. Johnson recites that "about 1653" fifteen settlers, being refused citizenship in New Netherlands, received Maryland permission to go there. Governor Printz had sailed for home and his son-in-law, Papegoja, despatched Indians to bring back the departing fifteen. A battle ensued at some unknown point in the interior, and the Indians came back to Fort Christina with two scalps. Presumably the other settlers escaped safely into Maryland. The leader of this party was Gotfried Harmer. The official records of the "Proceedings of the Council" of Maryland shows that "Gothofrid Harmer" was one of seventeen Swedes and Finns who were made naturalized citizens of Maryland on July 20, 1661. Four Dutchmen and one Frenchman were naturalized ten days later.

A LETTER

FROM

William Penn

Poprietary and Governour of

PENNSYLVANIA

In America,

TO THE

COMMITTEE

OF THE

Free Society of Traders

of that Province, residing in London.

CONTAINING

A General Description of the said *Province*, its *Soil, Air, Water, Seasons* and *Produce*, both Natural and Artificial, and the good Encrease thereof.

Of the *Natives* or *Aborigines*, their *Language, Customs* and *Manners, Diet, Houses* or *Wigwams, Liberality, easie way of Living, Physick, Burial, Religion, Sacrifices* and *Cantico, Festivals, Government*, and their order in *Council* upon Treaties for Land, &c. their *Justice* upon *Evil Doers*.

Of the *first Planters*, the *Dutch, &c.* and the *present Condition* and *Settlement* of the said *Province*, and *Courts of Justice, &c.*

To which is added, An Account of the CITY of

PHILADELPHIA

Newly laid out.

Its Scituation between two Navigable Rivers, *Delaware* and *Skulkill*,

WITH A

Portraiture or Plat-form thereof,

Wherein the Purchasers Lots are distinguished by certain Numbers inserted, directing to a Catalogue of the said Purchasers Names

And the Prosperous and Advantagious Settlements of the *Society* aforesaid, within the said City and Country, &c.

Printed and Sold by Andrew Sowle, *at the Crooked-Billet in* Holloway-Lane *in* Shoreditch, *and at several Stationers in* London, 1683.

---

they move by the Treaties for Land, iddle of an half , or at a little d their business, the Name of his King *to speak to* the King's mind. ; he feared, there t was the Indian that if the Young y. Having thus dispose of, and files, not buying ved to *whisper* or le, but *fervently*, em without the me of *Wise*, that hase was agreed, the Indians and made a Speech to us done; next, ace with me, and that no Governour ed them well, they and said, *Amen*,

, be it *Mariber* d to the quality a Woman, they cannot do. 'Tis the Dress, and

end the matter: that they are the dition for ill, and dition looks, the estation: What t between Good, to out-live the Will of God; for conscience, while

, of the stock of and not planted or ded that extrait is not imposica. In the next nce, that a man ent. But this is they have a kind Mourning a year,

So much for the *Natives*, next the *Old Planters* will be considered in this Relation, before I come to our *Colony*, and the Concerns of it.

XXVII. The *first Planters* in these parts were the *Dutch*, and soon after them the *Sweeds* and *Finns*. The *Dutch* applied themselves to *Traffick*, the *Sweeds* and *Finns* to *Husbandry*. There were some Disputes between them some years, the *Dutch* looking upon them as *Intruders* upon their Purchase and Possession, which was finally ended in the *Surrender* made by *John Rizeing*, the *Sweeds* Governour, to *Peter Styresant*, Governour for the *States* of *Holland, Anno* 1655.

XXVIII. The *Dutch* inhabit mostly those parts of the *Province*, that lie upon or near to the *Bay*, and the *Sweeds* the *Freshes* of the River *Delaware*. There is no need of giving any Description

Facsimile of William Penn's letter of 1683, referring to Swedes and Finns.
Courtesy, Library of Congress.

The lapse of years between the flight from Delaware and the naturalization may be accounted for in many ways. As probable as any is the fact that the government of Maryland changed hands repeatedly during the period from 1645 to 1658 while Parliament was battling with the crown in England, and authority was not restored to the Calverts by Cromwell the Protector until the latter year.

Harmer and his party were not necessarily the first of the Swedes to move to Maryland. Andrew Hanson, John Erickson and Andrew Anderson may have been there on April 5 of 1652. Under that date these three subscribed to the certificate of allegiance of sixty-six residents of Kent Island to "the Commonwealth of England without King or House of Lords," but they may have signed later than the document was dated. We find no record of the movement of these men from Delaware. Andrew Hanson was at Tinikum Island in 1646, because his infant daughter was the first person buried there in the churchyard of the house of worship built by Governor Printz and presided over by Rev. John Campanius. Andrew, then spelled Anders, is listed earlier as employed on the farm of Mans Kling, along with Axel Stille. Axel was one of those naturalized in Maryland in

1661. These fragments of the early records are repeated here only as an indication that much is known, and much unknown, about the migrations into Maryland. The scholarly works hitherto referred to have sought out such facts in much detail, but the assembling of every list and roster which has been preserved leaves many gaps, many unanswered questions.

Whatever the movement westward during the Swedish ascendancy upon the Delaware, a new migration was promoted through the conquest of New Sweden by the Dutch. Johan Rising, the last Swedish governor, had instructed some settlers on the Christina River to lay the foundations for a high road to Elk River and the Chesapeake. At about the same time, 1654, he seems to have asked Commander Lloyd for the return of the Harmer party. His road, however, or so much of it as was constructed, was not to serve for the return of those departed settlers, but as a pathway after 1656 for the migration of other Swedes.

Rising had come to his new tasks with well determined plans for Sweden's colonial expansion. His first act on the Delaware was to drive the Dutch out of Fort Casimir. A little later Lloyd and the Commissioners from Maryland called at Fort Christina to discuss the boundary. The record of those discussions is lengthy, Rising being something of a lawyer and justly proud of his official papers. Lloyd seems to have begun with the natural claim that Charles I gave to the first Lord Baltimore the whole of present Delaware as part of the feudal state of Maryland. As the Parliament then in power, which Lloyd and his commissioners represented, had but recently cut off the head of Charles the First, this reliance upon his grant was not carried to any extreme contentiousness. Maryland, now a Puritan state, was ready to be friendly with its Lutheran neighbors. Johan Rising was friendly to the English, but he had no idea of limiting New Sweden to the area later to be known as Delaware. The meeting led to no solution. A year later New Sweden had been taken over, bag and baggage, by Peter Stuyvesant, and more and more Swedish settlers rolled up their few possessions and set off on the Elk River trail. No doubt some of them became settlers on lands which Rising could have argued were a part of the New Sweden, but which then and thereafter remained a part of Maryland.

It seems reasonably certain that the first Scandinavians to settle in Maryland found homes on Kent Island, regardless of the exact year of their

arrival. There stood the earliest settlement on
the Chesapeake, and the first one to be reached
by travellers from the north and east. Claiborne
had a trading post there before Maryland was presented by King Charles to his friend Calvert, and
Calvert's son found the Virginian an exceedingly
bad neighbor. Claiborne denied the right of any
king to cede Kent Island to any one, and kept up
his annoyance of the Calvert settlers at St. Mary's
until 1638, when Calvert moved up in force and
took over the obstructive settlement.

This might have settled the matter had not the
Puritan rebellion been getting underway in England. In 1643 a group of Puritans were exiled
from Virginia and Calvert permitted them to settle at what they named Providence, the site of present Annapolis. Religious tolerance had been a
fixed tenet of the first Lord Baltimore, but within
a few years the land of Maryland ceased to be in
any sense a sanctuary for persecuted Catholics.
The Catholics seem to have carried their tolerance
for the Protestants to the unhappy point of wel-
coming a majority of the latter faith, and then to
have discovered that a Puritan could accept tol-
eration, but not extend it.

By 1645 the Parliament in England was at war
with Charles the First. At this juncture William

Claiborne returned to Maryland, accompanied by Captain Richard Ingle, who said that he had letters of authority from Parliament. Be Captain Ingle patriot or pirate, he brought large force of arms. Seizing the colonial capital at St. Mary's, he gave Kent Island back to Claiborne. Leonard Calvert found help in this emergency in Virginia. The fortunes of war, and of diplomacy, waged back and forth, the Commissioners of Parliament officially taking charge in 1654. Meanwhile, in 1650, Anne Arundel County was created around Providence (Annapolis) and Charles County to north and west of St. Mary's. Both were settlements of Protestants. In both were a few Scandinavian families which had come by way of Kent Island. Others were in St. Mary's and Calvert counties, and it may be that the Lutherans practiced more tolerance in religious matters than some of their neighbors. At any rate, they were equally willing to go along with the Proprietors or the Parliament party if allowed their own reasonable freedom of religion and their chance to cultivate the land.

Randle, or Randolph, Hanson, a brother of Andrew of Kent Island, followed a military career and had early joined forces with the Lord Proprietor. John, the youngest of the Hanson brothers, had gone almost at once from Kent Island on into Calvert and St. Mary's counties, had performed enough military service to be accorded the title of Colonel, either by fact or courtesy, and was one of the first settlers in the new Charles County. John had seven children, and his son Samuel had ten, most of whom married English husbands and wives and thus became part of the oldest families of Maryland. The history of the Hanson family having been remarkably well traced and preserved by the efforts of later generations, is worth considerable attention for itself, and may be regarded as typical of the more educated families among the Scandinavian colonists.

The early documents of every colony are full of "marks" made by settlers who could not sign their names. That there were illiterates among the Swedes in Delaware and Maryland is a reflection of the times, but no reflection on the race. It was true of the British and the Dutch and the French who came to the new world. Likewise, in varying proportions there came to most of the early colonies indentured servants, working out their "time," and harassed debtors flying from the imprisonment which was their fate in many lands. None of the North American settlements were penal colonies, but there were occasions when European powers sent over numbers of "undesirables," whose offences frequently were no more serious than religious nonconformity. Among the Scandinavians, and especially the Finns, a number of the pioneers were "burners." This designation arose from a Swedish edict prohibiting the clearing of land by burning, and a Finnish stubbornness in following a custom of generations. To assume that settlers of this character were criminals is the most erratic of conclusions. They were industrious farmers of the most enterprising sort whose sole offence was a refusal to believe that burning off the brush would injure the fertility of the soil. Such matters being debatable, they maintained that their experience showed no such injury, and they probably went right on being "burners" in New Sweden or wherever else they carved homes from the wilderness.

In every colony the urge for education was early expressed, with public school systems rapidly adopted. Nevertheless, the caste distinctions expressed by the terms gentlemen, freemen, servant, and slave broke down slowly and sometimes painfully. Whatever their original status upon arrival in the Maryland counties, the four Hansons were men of education, and "gentlemen."

Chapter III

THE HANSON FAMILY

$\mathcal{G}$EORGE A. HANSON, A DE-
scendant of the famous Maryland family, has
traced the lineage of his family back for many generations before Colonel John Hanson fell mortally
wounded beside his stricken king, Gustavus Adolphus, at the battle of Lützen in 1632. Gustavus
was succeeded by his daughter, Christina, and the
four male children of Colonel John Hanson became wards of the young Queen, although how
literal this guardianship should be considered is
not accurately known.

The Hanson who fell at Lützen was second
cousin to the King, his mother having been a
granddaughter of Gustavus Vasa, founder of a
royal line, and his father a young London merchant who had met Margaret Vasa while he was
travelling in Sweden, wooed and won her, and settled down there in the circle of the royal court.
The family tree of the English Hansons goes back

about two centuries from the John who wed a Swedish princess. The Vasa line surpasses almost any heritage in Scandinavian history.

It is possible that these four "wards of the Queen" possessed more quality than wealth, for if ancestral estates had fallen to their lot it is unlikely that all of them would have shipped off, in 1642, for the great adventure to the New World. Andrew was then about 25 years old and married, and William and Randolph and John all younger, the last named being a boy of 12. They sailed with Johan Printz, newly appointed Governor of New Sweden and a former army officer who may very well have been companion in arms to their father in the great days of Gustavus Adolphus.

Something of Printz's voyage has been told, his landing at Fort Christina, the freshening influence of new settlers and virile direction in the life of the little colony. When the new Governor chose Tinicum Island as his place of residence and colonial capitol he brought the Hanson boys with him to that location. Of their services and duties in the settlement or at the "court" of Printzdorf we lack any adequate record. It is probable that their family background and the youth of some of them gave them early advantages. Whether Andrew is the same Andrew Hanson, freeman, who once worked as a farm hand for Mans Kling must be a matter of conjecture. Certainly three of the young men ultimately became farmers, or "planters" in Maryland, and they must have learned something of that vocation. Randolph became a soldier, and may have had some military training under Printz. The total forces of the Governor, however, never numbered much more than a good platoon in times of peace. There were two, three, and perhaps at times four or five forts and blockhouses, but a "garrison" on that frontier was eight or ten soldiers and one commissioned officer, or perhaps a sergeant.

The wife that Andrew Hanson brought with him from the fatherland was named Annika, or Amika. Spelling of proper names was no exact science in those days. We have noted that their daughter Catherine was buried in New Sweden. Other children were born to the couple there. When Andrew died at Kent Island in 1655 there were three surviving children, and a fourth was born soon after the father had passed away. Among the four Amika made distribution of the father's property, the records of this act being among the oldest court proceedings to be found in eastern Maryland. The widow was then still a young woman, and later took another husband.

Some time between 1646 and 1653 Andrew had removed from the Swedish colony to Maryland. It is almost certain that his three brothers made this journey with him, and with Amika and the children. We may safely say that they went with full approval of their friend, the Swedish Governor, and it is more than probable that Printz confided to them his own misgivings about the future of New Sweden and his repeated but futile appeals for troops and settlers, and efforts to have a new governor sent out there to succeed him.

Apparently all of the Hansons went first to Kent Island, and the eldest brother made his home there from that time forward to his death. That other Swedes were located there is more than probable. In 1655 there is another record of three Scandinavian planters, Andrew Hanson, Valerus Leo, and Swan Swanson, operating at Kent Island. There are records also of a growing contact between the settlements along the Delaware and their neighbors in Maryland. Now and then a few trades in live stock were negotiated, usually with the Marylanders sending cows to New Sweden in exchange for horses. One Swedish writer speaks of such trades with Thomas Ringgold, and with Thomas Marsh, the "richest man in the colony." Ringgold was a signer of the oath of 1652.

When the Dutch had taken New Sweden and life there began to be complicated with too many regulations from New Amsterdam, more and more Scandinavian families crossed over the low divide to the waters of Elk River, and more and more new settlements developed along the Eastern Shore. A powerful Northern European strain was introduced into the pioneer blood of the commonwealth which was for generations to truly call itself the "free state."

The offspring of Andrew Hanson remained in the northeastern counties, his son Colonel Hans Hanson representing Kent County in the Maryland Assembly, and later Cecil County, and acting as judge in the former. William Hanson, third of the four who had come from Sweden, returned to Kent County after a short sojourn at St. Mary's, and remained a planter there until his death in 1684. If he had any children they did not grow to maturity, as he was survived only by Alice, his wife.

Meanwhile, the second and fourth of the brothers went on from Kent Island to St. Mary's, the capitol of the Calverts. Randle, or Randolph the soldier, and John, the young man who had come from Sweden as a boy of twelve, were to make even a greater impress on the history of their chosen land than Andrew and William. The theory that Randle Hanlon received preferments in the colonial service because of some influential connections, either in England or elsewhere, is scarcely supported when we find his commission as Lieutenant in the forces of Maryland signed by Cecil Calvert in 1662. While that rank carried more prestige and responsibility than in the armies of today, it cannot be said to have been gained by favor after eight or ten strenuous years of service on those frontier posts.

Randle Hanson appears with frequency in the records of the Council over a considerable period of years, reporting on all sorts of military duties from the major business of Indian fighting to the odds and ends of chasing elusive slaves, seizing illicit stills, tracing smuggled goods, arresting thieves, and repairing blockhouses. He became a familiar and respected figure throughout a growing colony. The marriage of his daughter, Barbara, to Thomas Hatton brought added prestige to his name, the Hattons holding their heads as high as any among the early Maryland aristocracy.

While his older brothers were thus variously making records of success and useful life, young John Hanson had gone on into St. Mary's County and as early as 1656 appears in Charles County, the

DANIEL OF ST. THOS. JENIFER
Signer of the Constitution
From portrait by Rosenthal, in Independence Hall

newly developing section centering around Port Tobacco where groups of Protestant settlers were clearing land and building homes. Within a few years he was a well known figure, was spoken of as "Colonel John Hanson," and had seven children: Robert, Benjamin, Mary, Anne, Sarah, John and Samuel. He lived to a ripe old age and saw much of the progress of his county and his colony into the early eighteenth century.

It was through John's offspring that the Hanson family spread most widely and added most liberally the blood of Swedish pioneers to the early family strains in Colonial Maryland. Robert, the oldest son, had a daughter named Dorothy who married Richard Harrison. Their son, Robert Hanson Harrison, was military secretary to George Washington during the Revolution and was nominated by Washington to the Supreme Court in later years. The oldest daughter, Mary, married John Briscoe. Mary Hanson Briscoe, a grandchild of that marriage, in later years married Michael Jenifer Stone, whose grandparents included Samuel Hanson. In such fashion did these large families of neighbors intermarry and the southern saying arise that everybody who is anybody is a cousin of everybody.

Numerous indeed were the children of Colonel

65

John Hanson's children. His youngest son, Samuel, had six daughters and four sons, of whom the famous John Hanson of the Continental Congress was the fourth. The oldest daughter married Dr. Daniel Jenifer and their son, Daniel of St. Thomas Jenifer, was a signer of the Constitution. Another married David Stone, descendant of a colonial Governor. The wife of Samuel and mother of this great family was Elizabeth Story.

Chloe Hanson, the youngest daughter, married Philip Briscoe of St. Mary's. Dr. Walter Hanson, of Harwood was the oldest boy. Samuel Junior became a planter, of Green hill. He did rather well at it, if his gift of eight hundred pounds sterling to General Washington for shoes for the troops was typical of his capacity for giving. William, another son, became Examiner General of Maryland.

We have mentioned a brief list of the Hanson family connections as they existed by the time John Hanson of Mulberry Grove was a young man. There were many more. The early eighteenth century was a gay, prosperous and happy time. Folks built their fine brick mansions on high land overlooking the broad acres of tobacco land, and visited back and forth. Paynton Manor was the Stone plantation, a house of abundant hospitality. Samuel Hanson, son and father of a John Hanson, died at his daughter's home there, in 1740. The Jenifers, the Briscoes, and a score of others had their homes among neighboring hills. And just across the Potomac some of the Virginia planters were flourishing and building, Lawrence Washington putting up a handsome place at Mt. Vernon a few miles up the stream.

Roads were steadily in the making, and new lands being opened inland from the bays and rivers. Prince Georges County drew its share of settlers and others went on into what would be Montgomery, while some courageous folks were risking the Indian peril farther west, far up the Potomac above the great falls. The land out there would be a county too, ere long, taking the name of Frederick.

Towns were growing too, and soon would be cities. Baltimore was founded, and soon surpassed all of the older towns. Ships no longer came and went at intervals of many months, or even years. Arrivals from abroad were weekly, and sometimes almost daily. There seemed to be no limit to the demand in Europe for the leaves of the tobacco plant, or for the furs of the wild animals of North America. The ships were larger, safer and faster and brought back articles of taste and luxury for the planters, when once they had brought only necessities and things to use in trading with the Indians.

Children of the rich planters were being sent back to Europe to be educated. Hunger and danger had been moved inland to the new frontiers, and the settlements along the seaboard were established places, with their courts and their judges, their fine brick and stone churches, their great plantations worked by many slaves, and their "first families" and "old traditions."

Men like Colonel John Hanson, of Charles County, who could remember leaving the old world in a leaky, creaky, wave wracked ship badly overloaded and overcrowded, and coming to a wilderness populated by a few tribes of savages and offering a tenuous chance for life and sustenance to the rugged and the hardy, lived to look upon a new and lively civilization, rich, radiant, and secure, and to see his children and grandchildren forming the strength and vigor of a growing country. It was a land well worth the long struggle which had brought it forward from its savage state. It would be worth the shorter, bloodier struggle which was coming, to maintain its liberties.

When the old Colonel passed away in 1713, at

the age of eighty-three, his sons were prosperous citizens of substantial worth. His will distributed additional lands for those to whom he had not made earlier provision, or who had not amply provided for themselves. He had much reason to look back with pleasure over a long successful life. Had he lived two years longer he would have seen the baby that was to carry his name to its highest honors, for it was on April 3, 1715, that his son Samuel had a son born at Mulberry Grove to whom the name of John Hanson was given. By that date Mulberry Grove was only one more of the number of fine properties owned by members of the Hanson family, its house one of the newer places on a hilltop overlooking Port Tobacco Creek. The baby John was but one more of the many grandchildren of the first John Hanson.

This lad would grow up like his brothers and his cousins, a stalwart boy loving the hunting and riding and games of the rich new land, going to England for a few years to school, returning to take a serious part in the business of managing farms and the growing business of politics. Before him lay a time that would be rife with politics and with problems, a time into which his background and his character would fit him for great service to his country.

Chapter IV

THE SPIRIT OF INDEPENDENCE
IN MARYLAND

$\mathcal{T}$HE AMERICAN REVOLU-
tion had many breeding places. Massachusetts was
the one where the first of the martyrs fell in the
Boston Massacre. Another was in Virginia. The
Randolphs and the Lees were not very different
people than the Adamses and Hancocks. Nor was
a Franklin in Pennsylvania or a Livingstone in
New York of different stripe. Where men of these
times met with men in whom their trust was
strong, brave words and wise words were said. At
no place were there more meetings of this character than in Maryland. At no place in Maryland
than in the group of houses centering on Port
Tobacco Creek in the southern part of Charles
County.

Here were the homes of Stones and Jenifers and
Hansons, Browns and Craiks and Smallwoods,
Mitchells, Briscoes, Howards, Thomases and Con-
tees. And here were ferry crossings of the Potomac

which brought the callers from north and south, travellers from all the colonies, men of affairs who kept close tongues in their heads until they sat in the old mansion houses among none but other men to whom they came well recommended. George Washington of Mt. Vernon was a neighbor and friend of these families. In after years he spoke of no friend so close and trusted as Dr. James Craik, who built La Grange near Port Tobacco, across the valley from his friendly rival Dr. Gustavus Brown of Rose Hill. Those two would be sent for on a solemn day in after years by messengers who spared no horse flesh. They were messengers from Martha Washington, telling that she wanted those physicians most trusted by her husband and herself. They sped to Mount Vernon only to find their knowledge and their skill inadequate to save the chief figure of their times and the most beloved of their friends.

Such were the friendships founded when these men were young and strong and given to looking straight at dangerous facts in a new world that was outgrowing an ancient order. Friendships founded in one of those corners of colonial America where the ferment of a national uprising was in the brew, founded among the mansion houses on the hills surrounding Port Tobacco

74

Creek in Charles County in southern Maryland. In a half dozen of those houses lived families of Hansons, sprung from those wards of Queen Christina who were among the early Scandinavian pioneers, along the Delaware and the Chesapeake. Into a score of other houses the Swedish strain had come by marriage. Strongly individualistic, not untouched with stubbornness, utterly resentful of injustice, able to endure much but to submit to little, it was a strain of character suited to the time and place. In the making of a nation it would play its part.

Let us look at the beginnings of this breeding place of revolution. If rivers are the mothers of civilizations there have been few greater than the Potomac. Winding slowly from its great falls, above present Washington, to its juncture with the Chesapeake Bay, it was an ideal carrier of commerce. Passing a land of gentle hills, abundant and fertile valleys, numberless tributaries pouring from the deep shade of hardwood forests, it drained a domain ripe for luscious agriculture. Captain John Smith had seen this when he first had sailed it. How the imagination of such early navigators must have thrilled at the prospect of these endless acres, sparsely peopled by a few roving savages, waiting for the home builders.

To its south shores had come the Virginians, step by step, up and up toward the head of navigation. To its north bank, the Cavaliers of Maryland, led by the Ark and Dove of the first Calvert expedition, settling at St. Mary's. From their vantage point near the juncture of the river and the bay they advanced in both directions, west and north. The first of the two establishments named Charles County was created at the north, for the colonists of William Brooke. In a short time this became, with new limits, the Calvert County of today, and the second and present Charles County came into being in 1655, along the Potomac westward of St. Mary's.

About forty miles up river from St. Mary's another stream empties into the Potomac. It had been named Port Tobacco Creek. Beyond the wide mouth of this tributary the Potomac, as you go upstream, swings widely to the left until the course becomes southwest for a short distance. As the swing reverses to the right, a half circle is described, and a great sweep of Maryland is half surrounded by the river. On high ground here, with an outlook down the broad river for many miles, Governor William Stone had taken up manorial rights. Across the mouth of the Tobacco the first of the religious orders had been granted

76

St. Thomas Manor. Manorial and leasehold properties had grown in number around the Port Tobacco inlet, and the shipping point to which the great tobacco hogsheads came rolling was at the head of navigation on the creek. There was placed the county seat of the fast growing Charles County, and there today a few crumbling old buildings mark what was Port Tobacco, a great center of colonial life for better than a century.

To appreciate the growth and change from the founding of the early counties to the time of the Revolution one must look for a moment at the system of land holding in Maryland. The deed from Charles First to the first Lord Baltimore was in effect an outright royal gift. Calvert "owned" the Province of Maryland as prince, potentate, and all but sovereign. For it he was to pay two Indian arrowheads a year, and each year renew allegiance to the British crown. Beyond that the land was his, as Lord Proprietor. A complete feudal grant, the great American palatinate. He could make the laws and administer justice, with power of life and death. Settlers would take the land on such terms as the Lord Proprietor might select.

The first compromise with absolutism was made immediately with the grant. A palatinate in a strange continent was of no value without settlers. To the first expedition was granted religious liberty, the right of law making under a veto power of the Proprietor, and land holdings either by manorial right or by what amounted to a sort of perpetual leasehold. The leasehold would pass by inheritance, and the rentals were in one sense equivalent to taxes, although paid as rental to the Lord Proprietor, or to the owner of a manor.

The manors were grants by Calvert to his friends or others, similar to the grant made to Calvert by the king. By custom, if not by law or edict, no manor was less than 1,000 acres, and many were much larger. One of the first, to Thomas Cornwallis at St. Mary's, was about 4,000 acres. With the manor went the feudal rights of lord of that manor, essentially ruling rights and the administration of justice, Court Baron and Court Leet. For a time in some parts of Maryland these rights were exercised, these courts were held. Court Baron for disputes between the lord and his tenants, and major crimes. At such trials the lord of the manor would preside. Court Leet for misdemeanors, and disputes among the lower classes. A deputy, a manager, an overseer might preside. The lords of early manors in Maryland were, for all but name, barons in their own right.

Very shortly this system fell largely into disuse. The counties took form, coming between the Proprietor and the manors. To the county was sent at first a ruler, called sometimes a captain, a commander, a governor. He too had, at times and places, judicial powers. With the disputes which shook the Calvert power, the Parliamentary wars in England, the Puritans at Annapolis, the Claiborne rebels at Kent Island, the deputizing of vice-governors by the Lords Baltimore, came the establishment of elected courts. Provincial assemblies passed enactments encroaching on the authority of the Proprietor, and not all of them were vetoed. At times there was no Proprietor or governor in Maryland to write a veto. With these changes in administration came changes in land ownership. The manors alone had been held in fee. Gradually the leaseholds became titles. The Calverts kept much of their power for many years, and held for themselves and their heirs many of the finest manors. But a thousand freeholders soon grew where but a score had been before.

There was settlement of many lands, and speculation in others. We remember Randle, or Randolph Hanson, one of the original four brothers who chose for himself a military life. In 1662 he was only a lieutenant, but in 1663 he leased 360 acres on the east side of Piscataway Creek "near ye land called Hansonton." This was far up to Westward, in present Prince Georges County, and already he or another Hanson had given a name to it. In 1667 the same soldier rented "Latchford," a 200 acre property in "Poplar Hill Hundred," probably from the holder of Poplar Hill manor. By 1691 Randolph was probably a rich old man. In that year he sold for 250,000 pounds of tobacco the land in upper Charles County called Lones or Jones Thicket. He had bought it in 1672 from Major Thomas Brooke. His daughter Barbara had married a Hatton and was certainly a rich young woman. West Hatton, the estate on the Wicomico, was not yet built, but other Hatton holdings were tremendous.

While soldier Randolph was thus accumulating interests in the land which he and his troops protected, young John Hanson had followed Governor Stone to the Port Tobacco country. There were subsequently a number of Hanson estates in Charles County, and there is some question at which point "Colonel John" made his first home. Wherever it was he settled down, he raised a large family, seven children being listed in his will. As his son Robert also had seven children and his son

THOS. STONE
Signer of Declaration of Independence
From Engraving by Longacre, after portrait by Pine.

Samuel had ten, in addition to the offspring of his other children, it may be seen that the Hanson blood was due to appear in many parts of Maryland and the other colonies. His brother Andrew's family was making its impression in Kent County and on the Eastern Shore at the same time that John's progeny were taking root in Charles. Randolph's progeny in Charles and in Prince Georges augmented the many other Hansons.

Colonel John Hanson was still living in 1713. His children were well established and his grandchildren numerous. More than that, his neighbors and friends on every side had prospered, the tobacco trade had made scores of wealthy families where pioneer settlers had made their homes in his earlier memory. The log houses of the middle seventeenth century had given way to stately and elaborate mansions, great houses marked by the tremendous double chimneys at each end which are still seen in many of the original homes, or their reconstructed prototypes. The crude furnishings of 1650 had been forgotten in 1700. No longer did the county records appraise men's estates as containing "one bed." Rich furniture, clothing, wines, silver, linens, silks and other luxuries came over on the tobacco ships, and the scale of living was considered equal to that in English country homes.

Population had increased manifold. Roads had been built, and the scanty settlements no longer clung solely to the water's edge. Trade between the colonies was developing, and stage coaches moved across the land. Factories had begun to appear, and the effort of the British Parliament to limit the manufacture of the colonies was sowing one of the seeds for future trouble. Colleges were starting. Churches flourished. Social life was finding expression in the broad hospitality of the plantation homes. Lodges were established, and members of the Masonic order probably spoke more freely within the secret precincts of the lodge those murmurings against authority which were beginning to be felt.

Books, and fascinating ones, have been written about the Mansion houses of southern Maryland, but none seem to have located any traces of the early Stone residences at Paynton Manor, or at Equality, or of the first Hanson homesteads which were probably on leaseholds of the Stone holdings. No doubt Robert Hanson inherited the home estate of Colonel John. That was at a date when men were building the first of those houses which survive in that part of Maryland today. Only

a few of those have weathered the storms of time
and the risks of fire. Samuel Hanson raised his
large family there in southern Charles County.
This Samuel for at least two terms had been a
member of the Maryland Assembly, and was both
Commissary and Clerk of Charles County for various periods. By 1750 he had been buried at
Equality, one of the Stone estates, but three of his
sons had handsome properties about the Port Tobacco scene. John was located at his birthplace,
Mulberry Grove, nearest to the county seat and
quite a show place on its hill overlooking creek
and river. Judge Walter Hanson was at Harwood, married to Miss Hoskins and raising a large
family. Samuel, of the new generation, was prospering at Green Hill. No doubt William, who
was to become Examiner General of Maryland,
had property of his own. Their sisters were married to a Stone, a Jenifer, a Lee, a Douglas and a
Briscoe.

To follow the family trees around the Charles
County of about 1750 is rather an amazing business. Dr. Daniel Jenifer, of "Charleston," for example, married a Hanson. His son, "Squire"
Daniel Jenifer, also married a Hanson, although
of a different wing of the family. And his daughter Elizabeth, married David Stone, whose first

wife had been a Hanson. It was a son of this couple, Michael Jenifer Stone, who married the Mary Hanson Briscoe mentioned in an earlier chapter. Amid such marryings and inter-marryings for two or three generations there may readily be some confusion. Perchance we had better leave Maryland geneology to its experts and be satisfied to know that there were Hansons or the kin of Hansons all about.

In the two decades before the Revolution the Port Tobacco country was at the summit of its prosperity and distinction. John Hanson, at Mulberry Hill, kept open house much of the time. This grandson of the lad who had come from Sweden in a leaky ship more than a hundred years before was a leading figure of the county, serving term after term in the assembly from 1757 onward. Born at Mulberry Grove in 1715, educated in England, and trained in the ways of the colonial planters, he was a handsome man in the prime of life, married to the beautiful Jane Contee, prosperous and respected. Only a few miles from Mulberry Grove was the popular Hooe's Ferry, most used of any crossing of the Potomac. Men of influence and position, travelling to and from Virginia and the south, stopped often at Mulberry Grove.

George Washington, the young soldier and planter, already with a reputation made on the western frontier, came often by way of Port Tobacco in preference to another road, and visited with Craik, and Jenifer, and Hanson, and Dr. Gustavus Brown of Rose Hill, and Thomas Stone, who was building Habre de Venture, the one of the Stone family mansions still standing on the Port Tobacco hills. Washington sometimes crossed from Mt. Vernon farther up the river and stopped by General Smallwood's place, on Mattawoman Creek, or maybe brought Smallwood with him, riding across the neck of land. The young soldier and surveyor from Virginia, friend of the Fairfax family, got about a great deal and saw a great many people. He was welcome company anywhere, and trusted beyond most men of his years. Will Smallwood was not, of course, a general yet, nor was John Mitchell from up at Linden. Perhaps none of them expected to fight anyone but Indians.

The Jenifers must have been there often, old Dr. Daniel and later the younger Doctor, his grandson. And "Squire" Daniel, and that restless bachelor, Daniel of St. Thomas Jenifer, full of study and book learning and theories of government and social order. These were the type of men who were meeting at Mulberry Grove and at Annapolis where one or another were sitting in the House of Delegates. Craik would be off with Washington to the Indian wars, and would dress the wounds of the dying General Braddock when that brave but stubborn soldier had defied Washington's advice and paid the penalty. What tales they would tell of that campaign. Hanson would be in the legislature when it debated the share of taxes which England sought to impose upon her colonies to pay for the French and Indian war. The colonies thought that England, winning all of Canada, could afford to pay the bill herself.

There would be talk over the long tobacco pipes around the great fireplaces about the restriction against iron manufacture in the colonies, and about the new taxes proposed in Parliament, and the effort to prevent colonial trade with the West Indies and other countries so that England might take her bit from all transactions overseas.

Then, in 1765, Parliament would pass the Stamp Act, a tax of stamps on every paper used for legal process. Court days were always big days in any county, but what a day it must have been at Port Tobacco when Judge Walter Hanson came riding down from Harwood to hold his court and tell the sheriff to serve his papers "on any old kind of paper," and to the devil with waiting for a supply of stamps. If clerk or sheriff quibbled about the risk of this, the Judge would tell them their more imminent risk was of going to jail then and there for contempt of his orders. Here was something to be thought about, and talked about. Did the Judge talk with his young brother John, the legislator? And his wealthier brother Sam, of Green Hill? And with others of the county? We may assume he did.

The Stamp Act had a hundred noses thumbed at it, throughout the colonies, and in a year Parliament found it a source of trouble but not of revenue, and repealed it. If fat King George and his fat ministers could have sensed the character of the colonies and their people, much good will might have developed from that repeal. Instead of that, the tax on tea was imposed as a gesture of defiance to the "tax evaders." Would the impudent colonials allow just that one little tax to stand, as evidence that laws were made in England and obeyed in English colonies? With a dozen voices in unison, the colonies defied by word and deed. They would do without tea. Followed the "Boston Tea Party" in Massachusetts, the burning of a revenue ship at Providence, and a tea ship in the Chesapeake. Committees of "Non-Importation" sprang up everywhere. There were Hansons on them in Charles County. Also there were Hansons on them in Kent and Cecil Counties, descendants of Andrew Hanson and his son Hans Hanson of Kimbolton, on the Eastern Shore.

So the yeast of revolution was fermenting. Not the ferment of the "have nots" against the "haves," but the ferment of men of family, worth and substance, judges and legislators, colonels and captains, planters and merchants. Not the desperate and the down trodden, but the dominant and the secure, owners of broad acres and many slaves, husbands of fair women who graced the tables of fine mansions. Not men with a grievance but men with an ideal, who had seen a great and prospering land develop under the principles of justice and fair dealing and were unwilling to see any departure from those principles. Men who knew how a civilization was made by men, toiling against nature, fighting against savages, dealing fairly with one another, making their own even handed justice, paying their own bills, defending for themselves that which their own work had built. Why should they surrender one jot of this to the scheming of a minister near the distant throne of the third Hanoverian George?

In the midst of these times and these events,

John Hanson of Mulberry Grove took a remarkable step. He moved himself and his family far from Port Tobacco's hills into a new home in the growing western area called Frederick County. He took this step in 1773, almost on the eve of the Revolution, and at a time when he was fifty-eight years of age. It is interesting to speculate about the motives which inspired him.

A purely business, or economic motive, is conceivable. Perhaps John Hanson was the first of the great tobacco planters to foresee both a decline in the tobacco trade through too great production, and a decline in the fertility of lands too long sapped of their strength by single cropping. Possibly the wisdom of his years had showed him that distant day when Port Tobacco, the great center of trade and wealth near the Potomac, would be a tumbled down, weed grown, abandoned village. Such foresight is hardly probable, however, for while there were declines in the prosperity of the tobacco barons in years ahead, the real downfall of the business came only with the Civil War, an event then three quarters of a century off.

Perhaps the Charles County planter also foresaw greater opportunities for his children in the newer region to the west, chances for new industry, diversified crops on fresh cleared lands, speculative prospects arising from the rapid growth of population. Much of this undoubtedly he did see, and rightly, yet it would have been an easier thing to have sent out to the west his grown and able son, Alexander Contee Hanson. Why should the established master of Mulberry Grove go forth himself, in the latter period of life, to the new county? The answer may be found with equal probability in the field of politics and statecraft as in the field of business. John Hanson may have moved to Frederick County in 1773 because it appeared timely to have an older, wiser head leading the political affairs of the new and growing west.

Frederick County was the fastest growing section of the state. There had been an influx of German immigrants, coming through Pennsylvania and heading southward toward the Carolinas, who had stopped to take up farms in the lovely valley of the Monacacy. There had been westward trends from tidewater counties in Maryland. Iron ore had been found in the western hills and furnaces set up. A new trade route, north and south, came down from Lancaster and York, through Frederick Town and Hagerstown and on to the Shenandoah and the Valley of Virginia.

90

Already Frederick was astir for liberty. Colonel Thomas Cresap, soldier with Washington in the western wars, member of the land speculative "Ohio Company" with George Washington and others, was leader of the "Sons of Liberty" at Frederick. Their mock funeral for the burial of the Stamp Act had been the greatest celebration ever witnessed in the county. They had resolved in opposition to the taxes for support of the established church, and they were hunters, trappers and soldiers of no common sort, pushing the frontier ever westward along the route to the Ohio, the great National Trail which was leading to the west.

In 1771, two years before he moved to Frederick, John Hanson was appointed deputy surveyor for Frederick County. It was one sign that men in control of events in Maryland were turning their attention to the west. Hanson remained a member of the House of Delegates for Charles until 1773, and when he did remove to Frederick was almost immediately returned to that august assembly from his new county. Within a few months of his arrival he was presiding at most of the public meetings in the county. Here was a man of mature years, long political experience, close friendship with leaders throughout the state, and possessed of substantial wealth. The younger men of the new county adopted his leadership almost instantly when he appeared among them. It would seem almost that his coming had been planned, that the way had been prepared. Were the understandings reached at many a gathering among the friends and neighbors on the hills near Port Tobacco, at visits to and from Mt. Vernon, at long evenings during legislative sessions at Annapolis, bearing fruit in the selection of John Hanson to take the leadership required in the growing west?

Whether Hanson's move to Frederick was politically deliberate may remain a question. That it was politically effective can not be doubted. Overnight, on the eve of great events, the growing county found her elder statesman. Charles County had other Hansons, and other Craiks and Jenifers, Mitchells and Stones. Other Counties had their Carrolls, their Pacas, their Chases. Frederick County could now match any or all of them in the councils of the province, and could give to Maryland a leader that Maryland could give to the coming Union.

Chapter V

WAR AND THE EMERGENCE OF HANSON

$\mathcal{T}$HERE IS A TIMING IN the careers of certain men, a joining of two periods in their lives, a period of preparation and a period of realization. The transition from the first to the second appears to be an accident. It is often said that when the event requires it, a man is found. We do not know to any certainty if such things are planned or merely happen.

Three years before he became President of the United States, Grover Cleveland was scarcely known to any American outside his home in Buffalo. Within his own orbit he was well and favorably known. He had been elected to public offices and served with skill and faithfulness each public trust. He had no reason to anticipate any future but a successful law practice as a leader at the local bar. Reluctantly he agreed to run for Mayor. In succession almost breathless he was mayor, governor, president, the idol of his party and his people.

Calvin Coolidge was elected, over and over again, to public office in his home of Northampton and his state of Massachusetts. Beyond those confines his name was seldom heard. He was a quiet, simple man, a good, steady, reliable politician. An event arose, the Boston police strike, calling for a man. Coolidge took the helm. Within a year he was vice-president of the United States, within three years, President.

Men of this sort appear to move toward destiny. At a certain point, determined as by accident, they emerge from the mass which is oblivion and move suddenly, quickly forward to the heights. This emergence is not in any way a change in the man. He has been prepared to meet events, and when the event comes, he meets it, naturally, almost inevitably. The emergence is not in him, but in the recognition of him by the people. The mass is a thing of great inertia. For years it will not see a man at all. Suddenly it will see him in a great light. Napoleon fired a cannister of grape shot from the steps of St. Roche, and became known to the masses. Lincoln joined in the debates with Douglas, and a great man emerged.

When John Hanson moved to Frederick County and assumed a leadership in the events of Revolution, a character of consequence emerged on the

JOHN HANSON
From Portrait by Hesselius, in possession of Mrs. Robert H. Stevenson, Jr.,
Boston, Mass.

American scene. The stage had been well set. He had been a member of the Association of Maryland Freeman since 1769. He was not a reckless firebrand, a leader of groups that shouted, sang, and burned in effigy the figures of the Lord North or of his tax collectors. He was a politician but not an orator. He had opposed oppression from abroad, but had never publicly uttered a word for separation from the British crown. He was ripe in years, full of patience, and stubborn only when it was needful to be stubborn for the right. He would be slow to take a desperate position. If he took one, younger men would trust and follow him. It was 1773, the year of the Boston Tea Party. Within a twelve-month followed the closing of the port of Boston, the alteration of a colonial charter by act of Parliament, the imposition of a military governor on Massachusetts.

On June 20, 1774 there was a mass meeting at the Frederick Court House. John Hanson presided. Resolutions were adopted declaring that the cause of Boston was the cause of all the colonies, and that no imports or exports with England should be conducted until Boston was relieved. Frederick would co-operate with other counties of Maryland, and urged Maryland to join with other colonies of America. There would be a moratorium on suits for debt in Frederick County while the boycott lasted. And delegates, headed by John Hanson, would attend a "General Congress" at Annapolis. Meanwhile two hundred pounds sterling was subscribed for relief of the poor in Boston.

Two weeks later there was a meeting at Elizabeth Town, which advocated all that had been stated at Frederick and went farther to advise a "general congress" of all of the colonies. After the meeting there was a burning in effigy of Lord North and a public burning of a chest of tea, by the unhappy merchant who had imported it, and who marched, bareheaded, torch in hand, to lead the burning. The people declared that they would make their own clothing rather than buy from England.

The "general congress" at Annapolis did send delegates to a "general congress" of the colonies. The Maryland "congress" grew to be called the Convention. It proceeded with a rare combination of courage and caution. The people of the colonies were Englishmen, as yet not thinking of a separation from the crown but only of asserting the rights and liberties of Englishmen, under the crown. A tea ship was burned in the Chesapeake.

Outbursts of this sort occurred in other provinces. The Convention kept its head and sought to treat with Governor Robert Eden, last representative of the Lords Proprietors. The Governor was lacking somewhat in authority and somewhat in understanding of his situation. By the end of 1774 a meeting in Frederick County said, by resolution, that it regarded the authority of the Governor as ended.

The same meeting discussed the organization of industry and the formation of militia companies. The term industry applied very especially to the powder and gun industry, the later as part of the iron industry. The western counties were preparing to defend themselves against the Indians. Or anybody else. Independence was still eighteen months away. George III could have compromised in Boston—could have compromised everywhere—but the term compromise would come more and more to mean outright concession. In other colonies they were organizing industry and forming militia companies.

In April, 1775 the British marched out of Boston to seize the arms of the militia at Concord, to break up the "organization of industry and formation of militia companies." Paul Revere rode to spread the alarm. At Lexington the first mar-

JOHN HANSON OF MULBERRY GROVE

tyrs fell. At Concord the embattled farmers stood
and "fired the shot heard around the world."
Probably something very similar would have hap-
pened if British troops had marched into Frederick County, Maryland. That county subscribed
$1,333 toward Maryland's quota of $10,000 for a
purchase of arms. A county government was
formed, called a "Committee for Observation."
It ruled the county until the formation of a state
government in 1777. John Hanson and his son
Alexander were members. John was elected a
delegate to "any provincial convention" which
might be formed. Thus his new county gave him
a blanket authority and trust.

At Annapolis there were men of many minds,
and much debate. Hanson apparently spoke very
little at the meetings of the Convention, but kept
his people in Frederick County organized and
prepared ahead of any in the state, and listened
carefully as men discussed this matter of armed
resistance. The "general congress" of the colonies
had met in Philadelphia and resolved that all
must stand together, in protest if protest would
suffice, in arms if General Gage chose a resort to
arms. While Annapolis was debating, Frederick
County was meeting once more, resolving that decisions of the Congress shall have the support of

all. Friends of Hancock and Adams could write to these troubled leaders on the firing line in Massachusetts, "what is said in Frederick is now felt everywhere." Maryland very soon had said the same.

Congress had named a General, and the General had ridden from Virginia to Massachusetts to take command of the troops at Cambridge, looking down on Gage's men cooped up in Boston. All of the colonies were to send troops. But when, and how, and on what terms? John Hanson had been patient of delay, tolerant of debate, while no instant peril loomed. Now he was back in Frederick taking action. Two companies of troops should march to Boston. Who said that they should march? The Committee. Who spoke for the Committee? John Hanson. The troops of sharp shooters prepared to march, without blankets, for it was summer, without food, because they knew how to shoot game, but with muskets, powder and ball. Whose troops were they, the troops of Congress, the troops of Maryland, the troops of Frederick County? All of these, but actually the troops that answered to the word of a man named Hanson, in whom there was public trust. He was sending them to the aid of his young friend and neighbor of Charles County days, George Washington of Mt. Vernon in Virginia, who was now the General. The troops led by Michael Cresap and Thomas Price started for Massachusetts. Up from Shepherdstown, Virginia, came Captain Morgan's troop, also marching to join George Washington. In twenty-two days these three companies of men had walked to Cambridge, feeding themselves en route, sleeping on the ground, singing as they went.

At musket practice they would hold targets in their hands. At long range they were accurate marksmen up to 200 yards. A British regular was inaccurate at half the distance. These were the first troops to join Washington and his army of New England Minute Men. Some of them would be with him on Long Island, in New York, in Pennsylvania, across the Delaware to Trenton and to Princeton. Some would survive those years and fight in later battles in the Carolinas. Lieutenant Williams, of Price's company, would end the war a general. Others would end it in unmarked graves. What was started in that summer of 1775 in Frederick County would be followed everywhere in Maryland.

The Committee of Observation was rightly named. Many things required observation, not the least important being the antics of the Tories.

Hanson wrote to the President of the Continental Congress, Peyton Randolph, in July 1775, asking for arms and ammunition for the barracks and arsenal at Frederick, sufficient to arm the male population in case of trouble with the redskins from the west. Already he had wind of the British dealings with the native tribes, the "Dunmore Conspiracy" which was in the making. He warned that Lord Dunmore, royal governor of Virginia, and General Gage were seeking to arouse the tribes in Ohio, Kentucky and Canada to devastate the borders of the colonies and lay waste the frontier settlements.

Patrols of minute men were established throughout western Maryland, watching the roads and trails. For months there was no result, but Hanson knew what he was looking for. On November 19, 1775, the thing looked for was found. At the home of Dr. Snavely, on the Conococheague near Hagerstown, four travellers were detained because their explanations of their business failed to satisfy the minute-man patrol. Protesting at the "outrage," the "three gentlemen" and their servant were brought, willy nilly, before Hanson at Frederick Town. Papers taken from them were also brought. John Hanson and Samuel Chase interrogated the prisoners. On November 24 Hanson could write to John Hancock:—

Frederick County, Md.,
November 24th, 1775

To The Honorable John Hancock,
President of the Congress.

Sir:—I am directed by the Committee of this County to transmit to you copies of the examination of Allan Cameron, John Smith, John Connolly, and a letter to one Gibson, from Connolly, and Lord Dunmore's speech to White Eyes, and a proposal by Connolly to General Gage for raising an army for the destruction of the liberties of the Colonies. Any orders relative to the prisoners will be strictly observed; the committee and the inhabitants of this County being determined to pursue every measure which the Congress may recommend to them as necessary for the preservation of these Colonies, at this time of imminent danger.

I am, very respectfully sir, your most humble servant,

John Hanson, Chairman.

The exposure of the Dunmore Conspiracy turned the whole course of negotiations with the Indians, some of whom remained friendly with the colonies despite the overtures which went on by the British from Canada and which won many

104

hostiles as allies of the red coats. That the whole aspect of the war was seriously involved is made evident by the haste of Hancock in communicating the trend of the affair to General Washington, to whom he wrote on the second of December, the day after he received Hanson's letter of November 24. From the nature of this letter it appears that General Washington had suspicion of some devilment afoot by Connolly, and a similar letter from Richard Henry Lee to Washington rejoices that "This wonderful man is now close in jail." The description of Connolly as "wonderful" seems to have been sarcasm.

Of the men taken with Connolly, the simple "John Smith" describes a character probably known to Hanson, in person or by repute. He is elsewhere described as "Dr. John Smith" and as "J. F. D. Smith," and referred to as a former resident near Port Tobacco Creek in Charles County. A very considerable tale of intrigue and adventure might have been written by the chairman of Frederick County's Committee on Observation, in place of the brief and moderate summary sent to Hancock. That the Congress was impressed by the result is evident in the official answer sent to Hanson:—

Philadelphia,
December 8th, 1775
To the Committee of Frederick County, Md.

Gentlemen:—Your letter of the 24th of November last being received, was laid before Congress, and I am directed to inform you that the Congress highly approves your conduct and vigilance in seizing Cameron, Smith and Connolly.

I do myself the pleasure of inclosing you a resolution of Congress, respecting the place of their confinement, and I am directed to desire you, in pursuance of said resolution, to send the prisoners, under guard, to Philadelphia.

I am, gentlemen, etc.

JOHN HANCOCK, President.

John Hanson had other work to do, endless work. A gun lock factory was built at Frederick. Barracks were erected. He was made Treasurer of Frederick County. He was back and forth to meetings of the Convention at Annapolis, listening while Maryland debated anew how far she would support the resolutions of the Continental Congress. In Mid-winter she instructed her delegates not to sponsor a final break with England unless the Maryland convention should advise it. Not until June of 1776 would the Convention alter this instruction. After many meetings, many questions, many words, a set of resolutions was proposed allowing Maryland in Congress to vote for Independence. John Hanson, of Frederick County, spoke only one sentence on the subject, but it was the last word of the debate. "These resolutions ought to be passed and it is high time." Thus it was possible for Maryland's men in Congress on July 4, 1776 to vote for independence.

Thomas Stone of Habre de Venture, near Port Tobacco, nephew of John Hanson, became a signer of the Declaration. Pennsylvania has long been proud of her "Swedish signer of the Declaration of Independence," John Morton. Morton was descended from Swedish and Finnish settlers on the Delaware, a straight line of male descent running back something less than one hundred years in the New World.

Thomas Stone was a son of more than one family famous in colonial America, but one line of his ancestry went back to that settlement on the Delaware when it was yet, a century and a half before, known as New Sweden. One of his great-great-grandfathers had been the twelve year old lad, John Hanson, who sailed out of Gottenburg with Governor Printz on the ship *Fama (Renown)*, a lad who was an orphan and a "ward of Queen

Christina." A lad whose father, a cousin of the King Gustavus Adolphus, fell beside his leader at Lützen. The blood of Swedish pioneers flowed in the veins of at least two men, Morton and Stone, who were privileged to sign the Declaration, a privilege that would carry their names onward forever into glory.

Chapter VI

A NATION IN THE MAKING

$\mathcal{T}$HE THIRTEEN BRITISH colonies whose delegates determined to help Massachusetts in resisting General Gage were not a nation. Under a variety of charters, patents, grants of power, authorities of royal governors, customs grown by habit into law, they were yet thirteen separate groups of settlements owing each its own allegiance to the British crown. In 1775 few men had yet given much thought to ending that allegiance The meeting of their delegates could yet be hardly said to be a Congress. They knew only that the people of these colonies had a common purpose, a common trouble, a common courage. Before they would submit to tyranny, these men determined they would fight. In order to fight they decreed to have an army, and to direct an army they must choose a General. This much was agreed to. What to do thereafter remained an open question.

Each event calls for a man. Here among the thirteen colonies there was call for a soldier, and the soldier was George Washington. Then in each colony, each county, each town and township, there was need of men. For this event John Hanson emerged in Frederick County, Maryland. Other men in other counties, in other colonies, men who were known among their fellows and upon whom their fellows could rely. Men who would be trusted in all things including life and death, trusted to lead into new paths and new commitments, to lead in a new cause to which we pledge "our lives, our fortunes and our sacred honor."

There was almost no real authority in the delegations which must nevertheless become The Congress. Each colony sent delegates, chosen as it pleased, instructed as it pleased. The whole group could meet, debate, resolve, and urge each colony to comply with things resolved. Then it remained for thirteen separate colonies to act. Each must send troops, commission officers, enlist soldiers for three months, six months, perhaps a whole year, and find the funds to pay them and the food to keep them in the field. Those troops would go to where the army was, and the army was where the General was. What rights or powers had the Gen-

MRS. JOHN HANSON
From Portrait by Hesselius, in possession of Mrs. Robert H. Stevenson, Jr.,
Boston, Mass.

eral? At the moment he had the supreme right of being the most able man. He knew how to act like a General, to issue orders that would be obeyed. Since he showed no sign of questioning his own authority, other men did not question it. He was the General of a flimsy little temporary coalition of thirteen scattered colonies, remote from one another in time and space, close knit together in a common cause, knowing nothing except to stand together against the tyrant, to set their General against the tyrant's general, to send their soldiers against the soldiers of the distant crown. A coalition without a government, without a king, without a bank or any money of its own, without an ally, and strangest fact of all, without a precedent.

How could this ungoverned thing become a nation? It had nothing that pertains to being a nation, excepting only one most important thing. That one thing that it had was men. The sort of men it had were the men who had stood up against the red coats at Lexington and Concord, the sort of men who had held court with unstamped paper, who had "organized industry and formed militia companies" by act of "Committees of Observation."

A group of boys meeting at play on a holiday

afternoon decide "let's have a club." They choose a leader. They decide to build a clubhouse. William Brown asks his mother if they can use the empty piano box in her back yard. Tommy Smith fetches some boards that have been lying at the end of Smith's garage. Jimmy Jones brings a hammer and some nails from the Jones wood shed. Presently there is a clubhouse. On this plan the United States of America would be built out of thirteen colonies, because there were men determined on the building of it.

Action in the Congress was by one vote for each colony, and decisions for a long time were by unanimous consent. The delegates of each colony looked to their own legislatures for authority. If the legislative bodies could not function because they lacked authority or leadership as it had come from royal governors, new legislative bodies were created, invented, assembled as might be needed. Assemblies, conventions, call them what you please, only let them meet, let them take courage and take power and give backing to the Congress, backing to the General. The organization of industry and forming of militia companies must go on. In this way the colonies carried on through 1775, standing firm outside Boston, negotiating through agents overseas with those in power in

England, preparing for more resistance if more resistance should be needed.

By 1776 much progress had been made, the leaders from each section had met in Congress, gone back and met in legislatures, gone back to Philadelphia to meet in Congress once more. Negotiations abroad had made no progress. The colonies were ripe for Independence, and so declared themselves. Having declared themselves a nation, they still had far to go in making themselves one, but for this task they were now partly ready and by 1777 the Articles of Confederation had been drawn, considered in the Congress, submitted to the colonies which were now states. It was at this point that a question raised itself, a question which grew larger and larger as its import spread, a question which through four troubled years delayed the actual making of a nation from its thirteen parts. The name of it was The Western Lands Question. The man who raised the question was John Hanson.

Briefly stated, the question dealt with the great areas of land lying west of the Appalachian Mountains and pertaining, by a variety of claims, chiefly to the colonies of Virginia, New York, Massachusetts and Connecticut. In the new nation, the United States, should these vast areas continue to be parts of the four claimant colonies, or should they become lands of the United States and the joint property of all. The latter view was taken by John Hanson, and presently by all of Maryland, and like any new idea projected against a background of tradition it found few sponsors at the start. Nevertheless it was a question, raised by men of standing and respectability, men of patriotism and strength and leadership; men who were helping hold the flimsy coalition of the colonies together and weld it into unity and power. A question to which, sooner or later, an answer must be given.

Through four years this question would be debated, preventing the complete formation of the Union, but not preventing the united colonies from carrying on together in the conduct of the war and the building of a government. The leaders from Maryland, as close friends and ardent supporters of Washington and the army as the men of Virginia itself, occupied the difficult position of striving with all their power to help in winning Independence yet being the cornerstone of the political opposition which was blocking Union until Union should be based on what they considered the only durable foundation of reasonable equality among the several states. To compre-

116

hend the full significance of the war of politics which underlay the war of revolution it may be wise to make a brief review of the land claims and grants and boundaries which had grown up in the settlement of the new world.

It will be recalled that when Peter Minuit made the first purchase of land from the Indians on behalf of the colonists of New Sweden, the western boundary of the purchase was not defined and might have been presumed to be the Pacific Ocean. Within a few years the claims of Swedish sovereignty had been wiped out and Holland and England in succession assumed whatever rights the Swedish purchases involved. The question of the western boundaries nevertheless remained, and the same question applied to others of the early grants of territory in America by European crowns, and early purchases from various Indian tribes.

The basic claim to land in America by European powers rested upon discovery and was shifted by acts of war and conquest. Great areas in the New World changed hands in treaties dealing with wars which did not touch American soil, and lines of demarkation long possessed a vagueness readily appreciated by glimpsing the inadequate map making of the early years. Purchases from the

Indians often were made less upon any granting that the natives possessed rights of any sort than upon the expediency of keeping them at peace. The Indians had practically no maps at all and very vague agreements among their many tribes governing the hunting grounds of each. In the last analysis the deeds received from them played no serious part in the partitioning of the continent but were used at times as talking points in boundary arguments among the whites. At times the tribesmen may have been persuaded by rival French and British leaders to go forth and battle "for their rights," but the rights adhering to the redskins even in victory were no more than temporary loot. Land rights went always to the winning whites.

The grant of James First of England to the Virginia colony in 1609 definitely stated the westward boundary as the western ocean and islands within 100 miles of its shore. Since Captain John Smith had then recently been authorized to pioneer a route to India by sailing up the James River, it is probable that the Stuart king had little notion of the geographic meaning of his deed. Even the northern and southern boundaries were uncertain, these limitations coming later when Maryland and Carolina charters fixed them. William Penn's grant was also without well defined limitations westward, and his southern parallel was finally to be fixed after many years by Mason and Dixon's survey. Add to these uncertainties the varied claims of New York, Massachusetts and Connecticut to western lands, and we had the beginning of what might have been the greatest land contest in history, which might have prevented the formation of the American union. Generations later Americans yet were prone to argue about fence lines, causing Abraham Lincoln to describe his neighbors in pioneer Illinois as "a very litigious people."

More than a century following the first grants by British kings, the colonies were claiming and making disposition of great areas far into the present Middle West. In time a series of royal edicts had limited some colonies to those lands drained by the rivers emptying into the Atlantic Ocean. Maryland made no claim beyond the Appalachian divide. You will find a little northern spur of West Virginia today, jutting up along the western edge of Maryland and resulting from final interpretations of the early claims. If Maryland had cared to trade the principle of nationalizing western lands for that little added strip west to the Ohio River, much history might never have been written as it stands.

The watershed boundary first applied to colonies having no specific charters for land farther west, and Virginia and other states continued selling lands westward of that limit. After about 1750 the British government assumed the rights to allocating western regions, and the era of the great land companies began. Lawrence Washington and others founded the Ohio Company, and gained a grant of 500,000 acres in the Ohio River valley. The assertion of their claim was one of the generating points of the French and Indian War. Benjamin Franklin and Thomas Walpole formed the Walpole Company and sought 2,500,-000 acres. George Washington was among the sponsors of the Mississippi Company, which bid for an equal area.

Meanwhile Charles II had made western grants to his brother, the Duke of York, which became claims of the New York colony, and other monarchs had made western gifts or sales to the governments of Massachusetts and Connecticut, including portions of the present states of Michigan and Wisconsin. Much of this land was actually in possession of the French, and much more was subject to overlapping claims. None had been surveyed. Areas larger than the state of Delaware were but white chips in the game, and doubtless many claims were made as broad as possible against the reckoning time when surveys and settlements should whittle them down to factual dimensions. Since very few of the claims asserted before the Revolution were to take final form in possession, it is not greatly material what merit each possessed, but it was of vital import to the colonies in their early steps toward co-operation that some of the colonies purported to extend far into the west and others had no hope or possibility of territorial expansion.

George Washington's expedition to Fort Duquesne (Pittsburgh) under orders from Virginia's governor to oust the French from the headwaters of the Ohio is sometimes credited with having started the French and Indian War in 1754. Unquestionably there were other points of friction, but most of them were points dealing with the frontiers of France and Britain in the New World. While the colonies gave substantial aid to the royal troops throughout the fighting which did not end until Wolfe had scaled the Quebec Heights in 1759, there were numerous elements of disunion among the English groups, one sector after another arguing that the colonies with western lands might very well defend their own frontiers, and not call for aid from those who could expect no part in the disposition of the spoils. Why should states well bounded and fast set along the eastern seaboard send their men to trail the Indians on far frontiers belonging to their neighbors? It was trouble enough that this incessant lure of lands should have aroused the savages and brought them arms and bounties from the foreign foe. Such was the talk in more than one assembly. When the French and Indian war was ended, the treaty gave to England all of Canada and full title to the area beyond the mountains so far as the Mississippi River. Such regions as had been listed somewhat doubtfully as portions of Massachusetts or Connecticut, far out beyond the point where waters drained into the Atlantic, began to have reality. For colony or company, the land prospects had a brighter look. Millions upon millions of acres of fertile soil, tall forests, unknown mineral deposits, awaited the coming of more Englishmen, areas greater than the British Isles, wealth that would be richer than the storied Indies. A stubborn monarch called George the Third ascended to the British throne and kicked the whole of this empire away forever.

A map is still extant showing the entire area

between the Great Lakes and the Tennessee River and between the Alleghanies and the Mississippi marked as "New York." There is an act of the New York legislature ceding all of this to the United States, but that came later. To much of this area undoubtedly Virginia had a better claim, and one which New York was not disputing. Massachusetts and Connecticut had grants running like solid stripes on a flag straight across from Pennsylvania's western boundary to Mississippi water, defined in aged deeds by certain parallels of latitude.

The Articles of Confederation, drafted as the first written constitution for the new United States, made no provision for any disposition of the western lands, thereby leaving these areas to the states having best claim to them. Neither was any provision contained in the Articles for the admission of new states into the federal union. So far as this first effort at a constitution for the United States was concerned there would have been a perpetual union of thirteen states, some tremendously large, some as small as Rhode Island and Delaware, the whole extending from the Atlantic to the Mississippi River. The area lying westward of the southern states was largely unexplored, but already land companies were parcelling out great areas presumably a part of Georgia, and North Carolina had begun to consider its rights to the land that would soon be Tennessee. Thus Maryland could hope for little comfort from the south when it proposed that all the western lands be federalized. Indeed it was a brave and daring gesture which the delegates from Maryland indulged in when they offered an amendment to the Articles of Confederation in this language:—

"That the United States in Congress Assembled shall have the sole and exclusive right and power to ascertain and fix the western boundary of such States as claimed to the Mississippi, or South Sea, and lay out the land beyond the boundary, so ascertained, into separate and independent States, from time to time, as the number and circumstances of the people may require."

Although this resolution received at the time only the single vote of Maryland, it opened the discussion which was to wage for four years, and paved the way to the formation of the new states which were ultimately to be added to the original thirteen. It is a little difficult today for the American mind to envision opposition by twelve of the thirteen colonies to any plan by which any additional states might ever be created. In 1777 it was equally difficult for the leading men of that time to conceive any scheme other than a nation of the existing states, with western territories, or colonies, belonging to such of them as had fair and just claims to far frontiers. If it is ironical that those who objected to colonial exploitation by Great Britain should themselves seek to be colonial exploiters, the contrast is no more strange than that a man should fight and die for liberty while keeping slaves. Had the land claims of 1777 been maintained, would later years have seen the residents of Michigan in revolution against an alien government in Massachusetts which sought to tax them without representation? Would the Battle of Lake Erie have been an Ohio Tea Party with western settlers dumping tariff burdened merchandise from New York into the blue waters? Would citizens of Illinois, led by a lanky woodsman named Abraham Lincoln, some day be seen chasing a stubborn governor from Connecticut and his henchmen as they fled for safety across the Ohio River to the domains of a friendly Virginia governor of a territory called Kentucky? Had the land question not been fought out to a finish by the stubborn men of Maryland at the beginning of the nation, some such imaginative episodes might truly have transpired.

The initial Maryland resolution was promptly

buried in the Continental Congress, and the more powerful colonies moved forward with the campaign for ratification of the Articles of Confederation with a clause included therein to provide that no state should be deprived of any territory for the benefit of the new union. Virginia, New York, Connecticut and Massachusetts led in squelching the strange idea propounded by the Marylanders. Georgia and the Carolinas also had their eyes fixed on the west. New Hampshire had a claim on lands that were to become Vermont. Pennsylvania seems to have shared the view of the majority. Rhode Island, New Jersey and Delaware, the smallest of the colonies, dickered back and forth over proposals by which the states with no hope of added lands would share somewhat in the revenues from western land sales, but some of them, especially Delaware, gave some support to the Maryland proposal as time went on. Yet step by step, the ratifications of the Articles were accomplished, Delaware being the twelfth to sign. Maryland stood out alone, her delegates under pressure from all sides, but firmly supported by her own assembly in Annapolis, where John Hanson from Frederick County had come to take a leading part. In the end the utter rightness of the plan to federalize the western lands was destined to make itself apparent, so that the little earnest band of men who stood firm on their resolution would see it vindicated.

Men of Maryland had to resist every sort of argument and pressure, accusations that in blocking adoption of the Articles of Confederation they were hampering the conduct of the war, assertions that Maryland was taking unfair advantage of her geographical location, spread out wide from east to west so that all channels of communication from northern to southern colonies must pass through her gates. On their side they had no dearth of argument. If Virginia, for example, could support her government by the sale of western lands, would not Maryland's people leave the lands on which they were paying taxes, for homes in a tax free Virginia? If the frontier was to be owned by but half of the united colonies, would the others support armies for defending them against the Indians? Were the land-rich colonies ready to be taxed, acre for acre, with the others, for the conduct of the war?

Backward and forward the controversy raged, in Congress and out of Congress, and then slowly the plan of federal ownership, at first despised and ridiculed, began to gain new friends. A conflict arising between Virginia and the Walpole Company won to Maryland some powerful friends in Pennsylvania. New York, harassed already on her western front by Indian troubles, began to feel less interest in lands farther west. The general experience of the war and the responsibility of governing began to teach the statesmen of the period that old ideas of sovereignty might not be perfect. The plan for a PERPETUAL union grew in the minds of men as the possibility of compromise with England faded. The Tories had departed in great numbers for Europe or Canada, and the thirteen states had found that they could live, fight, and win without them. John Hanson's forecast of a nation which would grow in area and numbers, adding new states to the nucleus along the Atlantic seaboard, was finding a response and understanding among his fellows in the Continental Congress.

In 1780 there were signs that the war was being won by the colonies. Early in that year the legislature of New York agreed to concede to the new and perpetual union its rights to the disputed western lands on such terms as the Congress should determine. With the solid front of the land claiming colonies thus broken, it was diffi-

Mulberry Grove Manor House, with interior view of fireplace paneling.
From "The Chesapeake Bay Country" by Swepson Earle.

cult for the others to hold out. In September the committee having the problem in hand reported to the Congress that it should urge upon the several states a concession of the western lands as proposed by Maryland. Basing its judgment on the necessity of establishing a federal union on a "fixed and permanent basis" acceptable to all the members, in order to improve public credit, support the army, enhance the reputation of the new nation abroad and promote tranquillity at home, the committee asked the Congress to resolve:—

"That copies of the several papers referred to be transmitted, with a copy of the report, to the legislatures of the several states, and that it be earnestly recommended to those states, who have claims to the western country, to pass such laws, and give their delegates in Congress such powers as may effectually remove the only obstacle to a final ratification of the Articles of Confederation, and that the legislature of Maryland be earnestly requested to authorize their delegates in Congress to subscribe the said Articles."

Within a few months the legislatures had acted and in the spring of 1781 the ratification was complete. An act of Congress had recorded the intent to form the lands which should be ceded in accord with the recommendation into "distinct Republican states, which should become members of the Federal Union and have the same rights and sovereignty as the other States."

Chapter VII

HANSON AS PRESIDENT

$\mathcal{J}$OHN HANSON WAS ELECTED
to the Continental Congress by the legislature of
Maryland on December 22, 1779, but did not take
his seat until the following June. The war was at
its height, the colonies beset by problems of every
character dealing with the conduct and support of
army operations, and the union unperfected while
the western land question beset the scheme set
forth in the Articles of Confederation. The move
from Annapolis to the national forum was not a
great one, for throughout the Revolution every de-
cision of the Congress, on major issues, was debated in each provincial legislature. Time and
again the members of the Congress waited for "in-
structions" from the State Capitol at home. Hanson had been active in this picture from the first,
managing the war activities in Frederick County,
carrying his county enthusiasm to the colonial capitol, debating at Annapolis the issues on which the

delegates to Congress must have support from home.

Not a great many of John Hanson's letters have come down to us, and it is probable that he was less prolific with his pen than many of his contemporaries. From the time of his arrival in Philadelphia, however, he wrote with regularity to his son-in-law at Frederick, Dr. Philip Thomas, and some of those letters have been preserved. About two months after taking his seat in Congress he expressed plainly what was in the hearts of the men who were striving to weld a nation and guide it on to victory:

Philadelphia,

DEAR DOCTOR: Aug. 4th, 1780

The account you have given me of my plantation affairs, and the plentiful crops in general, is very pleasing; the harvest throughout the country as far as I have heard is very great. No danger of our army wanting bread in future, if cash can be found to pay for it, but there lies the general difficulty. The States must principally be depended on, and they are extremely backward in their payments. The want of money will, I am afraid, embarrass our affairs exceedingly. Our army is in motion, a vigorous, offensive campaign in conjunction with our generous ally is intended, and

134

little or no money in the Treasury to carry on its operations; this may retard, but still I trust we shall be able to get along. A million of dollars is coming on from Massachusetts, and I hope the other States will be forwarding theirs. In my last I mentioned the sailing of the British fleet from New York, and that I thought their destination was Rhode Island. The event has proved I was not mistaken. They are now lying off Block Island, in sight of Rhode Island, waiting, it is supposed, for the troops sent from New York, through the Sound to co-operate with them. Whether they will be able to effect their purpose, which must be the destruction of the French fleet and army at Rhode Island, time will show. General Washington moved with his army on Friday last towards North River. It is probable he has crossed it before this time. The militia to the eastward are in motion. The Pennsylvania militia commanded by President Reed are under marching orders. Those of this town are to march the 10th instant, and I trust the troops from Maryland are on their way. In all probability the campaign will be bloody. God send it successful.

With great esteem, yours,

To Dr. Philip Thomas,   JOHN HANSON.
Frederick Town, Md.

Hanson's work had been doubled by the land argument, for his position on that issue made the whole status of Maryland a trying one. The need for close, quick, confident co-operation in the Congress in managing a war was very great. Maryland must give every help in this, while standing firm and for a long time alone against the field on the crucial question of the lands. To justify the stubborn courage of her "filibuster" on the single issue which blocked the path to a "perpetual union," Hanson felt that Maryland must always show an equal or greater courage, an equal or greater firmness, for unity and harmony in the conduct of the war. He was always willing that Maryland should do a little more than would be asked of her by Congress, that Frederick County would do double any duty asked of her by Maryland. Thus he came to the Congress to take personal leadership in the final struggle on the land question. He was not a new or unknown man among his fellows, but an honored and respected figure in whom every one had honest faith.

Here again he must do double duty, despite the fact that he was one of the oldest men in Congress. He could shun no task, avoid no committee meeting, neglect no obligation dealing with the business of the war. He must also be available to confer, discuss, persuade, to "lobby" as it were, for endless hours on the western lands matter. To all of this he gave in full his energy and strength, his forceful wisdom of ripe experience, his dignity of years and his untiring enthusiasm of ever youthful courage.

One letter to Dr. Thomas, in the early autumn of 1780, seems to have been written in the manner of a man who is expressing to his trusted confidant some thoughts which press upon his mind but are not suitable for free discussion. He wrote what was actually a series of questions, to which Thomas could have given answers but no solution. The letter is vastly illuminating of the problems before the Continental Congress.

Philadelphia,
Sept. 19th, 1780

DEAR DOCTOR:

Our army is still much distressed for want of meat. They get one meal only in three days, and how long that scanty allowance will continue is uncertain. The Jersey inhabitants, in whose State the army is, are plundered daily by parties of the army, without a possibility of constraint. Are not the worst of consequences to be dreaded from the armies thus caring for themselves? Will not the affections of these people who have upon all occasions exerted themselves in support of the common cause, be at length alienated from the army and look upon them rather in the light of robbers and enemies than the protectors of their rights? Is it not most shameful that our army should be starving and driven to such measures, while the country abounds with provisions?

Farewell, etc.

JOHN HANSON.

During the late months of 1780 the land fight was in the winning. On February 3, 1781 Hanson was elected to Congress the second time, taking his seat on February 22, a birthday not then celebrated. Probably Washington gave it little if any notice himself. He was preparing the campaign that would win the war and set up a free people. On March 1, 1781, the delegates to Congress signed the Articles of Confederation, all of the ratifications having been received. Says the Journal of the Congress:—

"March 1st, 1781:—According to the order of the day, the Honorable John Hanson and Daniel Carroll, two of the Delegates for the State of Maryland, in pursuance of the Act of the Legislature of that State, entitled, 'An Act to Empower the Dele-

gates of this State in Congress to Subscribe and
Ratify the Articles of Confederation,' which was
read in Congress on the 12th day of February last,
and a copy thereof entered on the minutes, did, in
behalf of the said State of Maryland, sign and ratify the said Articles, by which act the confederation
of the United States of America was completed,
each and every of the Thirteen United States,
from New Hampshire to Georgia, both included,
having adopted and confirmed, and by their delegates in Congress, ratified the same."

The event was celebrated widely, some writers
of the time forecasting that the date would be a
perpetual national holiday as the anniversary of
the founding of the nation. The confederation of
thirteen sovereign states had become a federal union, one and indivisible, and by the terms of the
agreement the union was "perpetual." Abraham
Lincoln had occasion in 1861 to refer to that word,
the pledge of perpetuity voluntarily accepted by
each state more than eight years before the adoption of the final Constitution.

While unity was being secured in the political
structure of the new government, progress was
being made afield. The British had sent Cornwallis to the south, to stamp out the rebellion in
the Carolinas and Virginia. Moving their troops

from New York by water, they seem to have concluded that they would easily outdistance Washington and his army, and presumably hoped also to outwit Rochambeau and the French fleet. Probably they underestimated the fighting qualities of the militia under Greene, and expected to move through the southern colonies with a minimum of resistance. It would be many months before the final outcome of this strategy would be known, but Hanson, at Philadelphia, seems to have been well advised and optimistic. He wrote to Dr. Thomas on February 28, the day before the signing of the Articles:—

Philadelphia,
Feb. 28, 1781

DEAR DOCTOR:

If General Greene can avoid coming to a general action for a few days, I think Cornwallis' army must be destroyed. The English ships are blocked up at Portsmouth by a 64 and 2 French Frigates. A detachment from the main army of about 1,500 men are on the march, commanded by the Marquis De Lafayette, destined for Portsmouth, their route by way of the head of the Elk, and from thence by water. It is to be hoped that the State of Maryland will give all the assistance they can in this enterprise. They have some armed vessels at Baltimore and Annapolis, and men surely may be had.

With esteem, yours,
JOHN HANSON.

To Dr. Philip Thomas,
  Frederick Town, Md.

Amid all these matters of high import, a member of the Congress had also his own personal and family matters on his mind. Farm lands must have attention, business must be kept in motion. Hanson wrote to Thomas on April 10, 1781, reflecting this phase of an extremely busy life:—

Philadelphia,
Apr. 10th, 1781

DEAR DOCTOR:

*   *   *   *   *

Should have left this place last week, but since the ratification of the Confederation, 9 States are required to make a Congress, 4 are unrepresented and my withdrawal would leave a number insufficient to transact business, which at this critical conjunction would perhaps be thought unpardonable. However, I hope to get away by Thursday next. Some absent members are sent for, and one from Jersey is expected in to-day or to-morrow, when the State will be represented.

Yours most affectionately,

JOHN HANSON.

To Dr. Philip Thomas,
   Frederick Town, Md.

The year 1781 was one of triumph for the new United States. Aid from the French had now arrived in substantial volume. There were French troops, and even more important, there was a French fleet to aid the Continental Army. By late summer Cornwallis would find himself bottled up in Yorktown, surrounded by Washington on land, cut off by the French from communication with New York by sea.

The progress of events was closely watched from Philadelphia. John Hanson summed them up in writing to his son-in-law.

Philadelphia,
Oct. 16th, 1781

DEAR DOCTOR:
   The British have repaired the damage received in their late engagements with the Count de Grasse, and have been reinforced with six ships of the line. Their fleet now consists of twenty-nine ships

of the line, which, from undoubted intelligence, sailed from the Hook about the 10th with 10 fine ships and upwards of five thousand troops for the relief of Lord Cornwallis, on whose defense or defeat the issue of the combat they think depends. This is a very formidable fleet, and though considerably inferior to the French, yet as so much depends upon the event of a second engagement, my fears are somewhat excited, The Count de Grasse and General Washington are informed of their approach. The former will, no doubt, be prepared to receive them, and the latter will be quickened in his operations against the beseiged. In a few days we may expect to receive advices of utmost importance. God grant they may be favorable to America. I am sorry Mr. Johnson is left out of the delegation. I wish with all my heart he had been in my place, conscious of his superior abilities to serve the public in general and our country in particular. Supposing a vacancy should happen, would he, do you think, be elected? I wish to be informed in this particular.

Affect.,

JOHN HANSON.

To Dr. Philip Thomas,
  Frederick Town, Md.

Even the elements were with the allies, and a storm delayed the vessels seeking to relieve the British general. On the 19th of October he surrendered to George Washington. A courier galloped by day and night up the Eastern Shore of Maryland, through Delaware and on to Philadelphia to tell the Congress.

There is a striking picture of the skill and tact of Hanson in his handling of his fellow men to be seen in the nature of his letter to Dr. Thomas on the event of the surrender. He wrote to his son-in-law "I congratulate you most sincerely upon the surrender of Lord Cornwallis to General Washington" etc. Thomas had been his confidential representative in Maryland since Hanson had moved to Philadelphia. The older man had asked a great deal of the younger, as he had of many others. Thomas had looked after farms and enterprises in Frederick County, and kept a hand in local politics. He had been often to Annapolis, urging on the state those steps of enterprising co-operation so greatly needed by the army and the Congress. Hanson had spurred on Thomas to spur on Maryland with help in moving Lafayette's troops southward via the Chesapeake, and reinforcing them. On October 23 Hanson wrote to Thomas:—

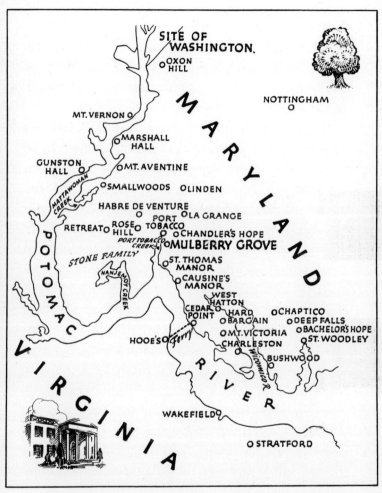

SITE OF
WASHINGTON.
O OXON
HILL

NOTTINGHAM
O

MT. VERNON O

O MARSHALL
HALL

GUNSTON
HALL

O MT. AVENTINE

MATTAWOMAN CREEK

O SMALLWOODS   O LINDEN

HABRE DE VENTURE
O   O LA GRANGE
PORT
RETREAT O ROSE O TOBACCO
HILL   O CHANDLER'S HOPE
PORT TOBACCO
CREEK
O MULBERRY GROVE

STONE FAMILY

NANJEMOY CREEK

O ST. THOMAS
MANOR

O CAUSINE'S
MANOR

WEST
HATTON
CEDAR O
POINT   O HARD   O CHAPTICO
O BARGAIN   O DEEP FALLS
O BACHELOR'S HOPE
O M.T. VICTORIA   O ST. WOODLEY
HOOE'S O Ferry   CHARLESTON

BUSHWOOD
O

Wicomico R.

MARYLAND

POTOMAC

VIRGINIA

RIVER

WAKEFIELD O

O STRATFORD

Sketch Map Showing Manor Houses of Potomac River country.

Philadelphia,
Oct. 23rd, 1781

DEAR DOCTOR:

I congratulate you most sincerely upon the surrender of Lord Cornwallis to General Washington, of which most important event we have information by a letter from the Count de Grasse, dated the 18th, to Governor Lee, and by him forwarded to the President of Congress by express. The particulars we expect to receive from General Washington in two or three days. The Count's letter is as follows: "I have just desired General Washington to send me back my troops, of which, probably, he will not longer stand in need, as Lord Cornwallis has surrendered. As soon as they are embarked I shall quit the Bay of Chesapeake, and endeavor to co-operate to the welfare of the United States in stopping, if I can, Sir Henry Clinton."

The British fleet sailed from the Hook on 19th, in the evening, and, as the winds have been unfavorable for them, it is probable the Count will get out before they make our capes, and, as his force is greatly superior to the British, should they come to blows the most favorable issue for us may be expected. The capture of Cornwallis, with the great number of vessels and the large quantity of British and West India goods, arms, etc. that must

145

have fallen into our hands, is a most capital stroke, and will tend more towards obtaining peace and to the security of our independence than the best managed negotiations. I was ever of opinion that no depredations upon the trade of the English—no conquests of their possessions in the East and West Indies, will induce them to make peace while they have an army in the United States and can flatter themselves with the hopes of conquering or regaining America, because it is probable they think that with America under their government they can easily regain what they may lose in any part of the world. Whereas, the total expulsion or captivity of their forces in the United States would extinguish their hopes and dispose them to peace sooner than anything else.

Affectionately,

JOHN HANSON.

To Dr. Philip Thomas,
Frederick Town, Md.

The brief letters which have been preserved indicate how constantly active was the guiding genius of his state's endeavor, and what constant aid he sought from relatives and friends, in driving on the common cause. Now with a word of glorious victory, Hanson quickly passes on the credit "I congratulate you." Let there be glory enough for all, and the will to effort kept ablaze. A month later he was writing to Thomas at Frederick:—

"I have written to the Speaker of the House of Delegates resigning my seat in the Legislature, which will immediately make public and, if Mr. Johnson will serve, pray use your influence in getting him elected."

Mr. Johnson was Thomas Johnson who had been the first Governor of Maryland under its independent constitution, 1777-79. The play of political forces had left this valiant leader in a state of temporary retirement from the active scene in Maryland. Hanson was seeing to it that his state again should have the service of the sort of man she needed. For himself he was seeking a way out of active public life when the struggle for freedom should be won. The victory at Yorktown brought to him the hope that his hour of retirement and rest might be at hand and he immediately set the wheels in motion which should make it possible for him to lighten, and then to complete, his duties. In this plan he was to meet delay, for almost immediately a new and heavier task was set upon him. The President of the Congress was Thomas McKean, who was also Chief Justice of Pennsylvania, and who would be called upon to hold his court on October 23rd. He had offered his resignation to the Congress for that date, but some one remembered that under the Articles of Confederation, in force since March, there was a provision for selecting the President of the Congress for a fixed term of one year in place of the former custom of suiting the selection to the times and convenience of the members. McKean was asked to keep his honors until the first Monday in November as provided by the Articles. On that day, November 5, 1781, the Congress unanimously elected John Hanson to its presidency. He thus became the first President elected for a definite, stated term.

In recent years a great deal has been made of this fact of Hanson's selection as the "first President." If some slight exaggeration has crept into the enthusiasm over this event it may have well been justified by the renewed attention drawn to chapters of our early history which have been too long neglected by the text books. A highly interesting volume, "John Hanson, Our First President," was written by the late Seymour Wemyss Smith and published in 1932. That studious work and its widely publicized reviews helped to arouse a warm response in Maryland, and a glowing pride among Americans of Scandinavian extraction everywhere. The true history of the Continental Congress had been long neglected, or if remembered had been too often written with false emphasis. Wemyss Smith, after prolonged research, struck out boldly against the notion that our government under the Congress, both before and after adoption of the Articles, had been incompetent. He made clear what all true students would appreciate, that the marvel of the times lay not in the imperfections of a new system builded under war conditions in a new land, but in the conquering of a thousand obstacles, the utter and genuine triumph of a people and their representatives building a democracy.

The detailed and technical position of John Hanson as "first" President of the United States in Congress Assembled, under the Articles of Confederation, while giving verve, sparkle and lustre to the work of Wemyss Smith and other writers, was perhaps actually of consequence chiefly as winning public interest to the factual history of the era. Dr. Edmund C. Burnett prepared for the Carnegie Institution of Washington a careful, scholarly bulletin issued in May of 1932 pointing to some errors of detail in the Hanson legend as presented by its warmer advocates. There were, in fact, a total of fourteen Presidents of the Continental Congress, some before and some following John Hanson. Payton Randolph of Virginia was the first. They presided over the Congress for varying terms, some for as much as two years, some for only a day.

Samuel Huntington of Connecticut had been chosen President on September 28, 1779, and was presiding on March 1, 1781, when the members signed the Articles of Confederation. He continued to serve until July 9, 1781. On that date Samuel Johnson of North Carolina was elected, but declined to serve, and may have been considered President for a day. On July 10 there was a new election by the delegates, Thomas McKean being then chosen. At that time the Articles of Confederation were definitely in effect. McKean, as we have seen, regarded the congressional presidency as of less consequence than his judicial duties.

Throughout the history of the Continental Congress, before and after the Confederation, the united colonies and the United States functioned through a government with no complete executive authority. All power was in the Congress and its committees. The growing need for the entrusting of real power to an executive authority was one reason leading ultimately to the adoption of the Constitution. Under the Articles slightly greater authority was vested in the President, and in a Secretary, of the Congress. This power, limited as it was, belonged to Huntington, to McKean, to Hanson, and their successors.

The assertion, then, that because John Hanson became President of the United States in Congress Assembled on the first Monday in November, 1781, for a fixed term of one year, and served in that capacity until November 4, of 1782, he was in reality "Our First President," is a statement lending itself to considerable debate. Many advance the enthusiastic claim that John Hanson, and not George Washington, was the first President of our country. In appraising the magnificent character of the strong man of Maryland, in evaluing his services to the United States, or in exemplifying in his person the contribution of the Scandinavian pioneers to the life and blood stream of America, no need for any exaggerated dictums can arise. The things that he did and the man that he was are all sufficient. His statue in the Capitol at Washington marks him, with Charles Carroll of Carrollton, one of Maryland's and indeed the nation's first Citizens. John Hanson himself was devoid of any exaggerated sense of the importance of the office to which he had been chosen. It probably never occurred to him that he was a "First President" or that his position was in any great sense an exalted one. He publicly fulfilled all of the requirements of ceremony suitable to the position, and privately had been in office scarcely one short week when he was giving thought to a vacation, if not a resignation. He wrote to Dr. Thomas:—

Philadelphia,
November 13th, 1781

DEAR DOCTOR:

The load of business which I have very unwillingly and very imprudently taken on me, I am afraid will be more than my constitution will be able to bear, and the form and ceremony necessary to be observed by a President of Congress is to me extremely irksome, moreover I find my health declining, and the situation of my family requires my being at home; I shall therefore take the first opportunity of applying for leave of absence, this, to yourself. The British fleet is retired to the Hook, and transports have been sent down from New York to take off the troops. It is probable the fleet will return to the West Indies. We

A Proclamation

The Goodness of the Supreme Being to all his rational Creatures, demands their acknowledgements of Gratitude and Love; His absolute Government of the World dictates that it is the Interest of every Nation and People ardently to supplicate his favour and implore his Protection

When the Lust of Dominion, or lawless Ambition excites Arbitrary Power to invade the Rights, or endeavour to wrest from a People their sacred and invaluable Privileges, and compels them, in Defence of the same; to encounter all the Horrors and Calamities of

Transgressions of the holy Laws of our God, and his past Acts of Kindness and Goodness towards us, which we ought to record with the liveliest Gratitude; think it their indispensable Duty to call upon the several States to set apart, the last Thursday in April next as a Day of fasting, Humiliation & Prayer; that our Joint Supplications may then Ascend to the Throne of the Ruler of the Universe, Beseeching him to diffuse a Spirit of Universal Reformation among all Ranks and Degrees of our Citizens, and make us a holy that so we may be an happy People; that it would please him to impart Wisdom, Integrity and Unanimity to our Counsellors, to bless and Prosper the Reign of our illustrious Ally, and give success to his Arms employed in the defence

THANKSGIVING PROCLAMATION OF CONTINENTAL CONGRESS

arrangements by land and sea, administer comfort and consolation to our prisoners in a cruel captivity; protect the health and life of our Commander in Chief; grant us victory over our Enemies, establish peace in all our Borders, and give happiness to all our Inhabitants; That he would prosper the labour of the husbandman, making the earth yield its increase in abundance and give a proper season for the ingathering of the fruits thereof; That he would grant success to all engaged in lawful trade & commerce and take under his guardianship all Schools and Seminaries of learning and make them nurseries of virtue & piety; that he would incline the hearts of all men to Peace and fill them with Universal Charity, and be-

benevolence and that the religion of our divine Redeemer, with all its benign influences may cover the earth as the Waters cover the sea —

Done by the United States in Congress Assembled this nineteenth day of March in the Year of our Lord one thousand seven hundred and eighty two and in the Sixth Year of our Independence —

John Hanson Presst

Attest Cha Thomson secy

Signed by John Hanson as President.
Original in **Kremer** Collection.

have no certain account of the French fleet having yet left our Bay.

Affectionately,

JOHN HANSON.

To Dr. Philip Thomas,
  Frederick Town, Md.

Three days later he had found that any immediate rest from his duties was impracticable, and he wrote again:

Philadelphia,
Nov. 16, 1781

My last was of the 13th, by the post, acquainting you for the reasons I have mentioned, of my intentions of resigning my seat as President of Congress, and accordingly, on Wednesday last, I desired leave of absence, but some of the members expressing their dissatisfaction at my so soon laying Congress under the difficulty of electing another, (for a difficulty there would be, as the votes of seven States are necessary and only seven States are at present represented). I shall continue, unless the assembly of our State should leave me out of the Delegation.

Affectionately,

JOHN HANSON.

To Mrs. John Hanson,
  Frederick, Md.

This letter was addressed to Mrs. Hanson, who was living with the Thomas family, and is the only letter of Hanson to his wife of which there appears to be any published record extant.

Thus did the simple and honest statesman decide that he must carry on his heavy tasks. That he would, within a fortnight, preside over the historic gathering at Independence Hall when Washington appeared before the Congress to receive its thanks for victory, apparently did not occur to him. Historic gatherings of that period had not yet become historic.

The year of John Hanson's presidency was an extremely busy one. Organization of the civil services of the country needed adjustment to the terms of the Confederation, for the Articles were, in effect, a written constitution, conforming to much that had been done before by general agreement, but differing in many details and broadening the tasks facing the young government. A Department of Foreign Affairs needed much organizing. The war, though potentially won, was far from actually ended. One of Hanson's first letters was to the King of France, to be borne thither by Lafayette, thanking our great ally for his share in the victory at Yorktown.

On November 28 the victorious Washington

came to Philadelphia, having stopped at Mt. Vernon for some days after the triumph at Yorktown. The Congress received him with some ceremony at Independence Hall, where President Hanson addressed him as follows:—

"Sir:—Congress, at all times happy in seeing Your Excellency, feels particular pleasure in your presence at this time, after the glorious success of the allied arms in Virginia. It is their fixed purpose to draw every advantage from it by exhorting the States in the strongest terms to the most vigorous and timely exertions. A committee has accordingly been appointed to state the requisitions necessary to be made for the establishment of the army, and they are instructed to confer with you upon that subject. It is, therefore, the expectation of Congress, that Your Excellency would remain for some time in Philadelphia, that they may avail themselves of your aid in this important business, and that you may enjoy a respite from the fatigues of war, as far as is consistent with the service."

To which General Washington made the following reply:

"Mr. President:—I feel very sensibly the favorable declaration of Congress expressed by Your

155

Excellency. This fresh proof of their approbation cannot fail of making a deep impression upon me, and my study shall be to deserve a continuance of it. It is with peculiar pleasure I hear that it is the fixed purpose of Congress to exhort the States to the most vigorous and timely exertions. A compliance on their parts will, I persuade myself, be productive of the most happy consequences.

I shall yield a ready obedience to the expectation of Congress, and give every assistance in my power to their committee. I am obliged by the goodness of Congress in making my personal case and convenience a part of their concern. Should service require my attendance with the army upon the North River, or elsewhere, I shall repair to whatever place my duty calls, with the same pleasure I remain in this city."

After this public and formal proceeding had been finished, another exchange went on between the President of the Congress and the General of the Armies. Hanson's portion of it is not of record, but on November 30 General Washington wrote to the President as follows:—

Philadelphia,
30th November, 1781

SIR:

While I congratulate your Excellency on your appointment to fill the most important seat in the United States, I take the same opportunity to thank you, with great sincerity, for the very polite manner in which you are pleased to tender me the advantages of your correspondence. As a mutual free communication cannot fail to be attended with great satisfaction to me, and will undoubtedly be productive of very useful consequences to the public cause, you may be assured I shall pay very particular attention to your letters. I sincerely accord with you in sentiment, that our public affairs at present assume a promising aspect, but suffer me to begin the freedom of our correspondence by observing to your Excellency, that, upon our future vigorous improvement of the present favorable moment depend the happy consequences, which we now promise ourselves as the result of all the successful events of the last campaign.

I am,

Your very obedient servant,
GEORGE WASHINGTON.

To the President of the Congress

It would be interesting to know exactly why this formal letter followed two days after the formal reception. George Washington and John Hanson were friends of many years standing. There is no record or indication of any break in that long friendship. There is, however, ample record that General Washington had not at all times held the Continental Congress in very high esteem. For years the Congress had addressed formal orders and demands to him, for years the same Congress had been unable to supply his troops with adequate food, ammunition or clothing, or to meet or compel the states to meet the soldiers' pay roll. Now, after one great victory with prospects of additional success, the General is seen agreeing to "a mutual free Communication" with the President of the Congress, a man in whom he has reason to have great personal confidence.

Was this a sort of treaty between the men in their official capacities? Certainly it indicates that heretofore the General had not enjoyed the "advantage" of free correspondence with the leaders of the Congress. Such personal co-operation is a new step. Two days earlier, after being publicly enjoined by the President to remain at Philadelphia and confer with a committee, Washington had politely responded that he would confer, unless the service (of the army) required his presence upon the North River, or elsewhere. One has a feeling, on reading those remarks, that General Washington was able to temper his enthusiasm for conferring with committees. But he appears, for all the stilted language of his letter, to have been pleased at the opportunity for genuine and frank exchanges with the wise old man of Maryland. With Washingtonian directness he begins the correspondence with plea for action, "vigorous improvement of the present favorable moment." George Washington seems to have cherished ideas for improving the moment by means other than long conferences with committees.

Undoubtedly John Hanson smiled over that letter from his neighbor of Mt. Vernon and Mulberry Grove days. He knew what Washington had gone through for five years past, struggling to maintain an army, to meet and defeat the enemy, with such indifferent backing from the half impotent Congress and often confused state authorities. He, himself had been complaining vigorously about it. He knew also what Congress and the legislators of the states had striven and coped with, apathy in some states, jealously in others, opposition by wealthy tories, friction within the

army mounting to actual treason in the case of
Arnold. All of this and much more John Hanson
knew from having lived it, wrestled with it, helped
to overcome it. He knew also that the war was
not yet finished, that General and Congress must
work in closer unison if possible, and that in his
love and friendship for the gallant soldier of Mt.
Vernon lay a means for tying them together for
the final effort. To this purpose, and the endless
tasks of his official duty, the old and tiring statesman from the Free State would now devote himself.

One enactment after another came from the
Congress during 1782. The finances of the new
country needed much putting in order. A national bank must be established. In the midst of
these many tasks there was great detail heaped
upon the President of the Congress. Already that
officer was becoming an executive, without relief
from the duties of a legislator.

As the spring of 1782 drew on, with a new campaign at arms facing the new country, it became
essential to revive the spirit of the people for one
final united effort, and to make clear that all had
not been accomplished by the victory over Cornwallis. On March 19 John Hanson, President of
the United States in Congress Assembled, signed

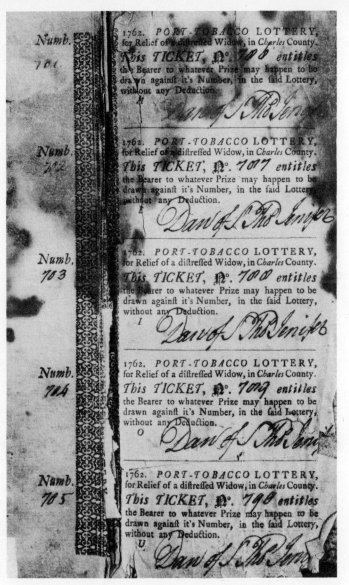

BOOK OF LOTTERY TICKETS: PORT TOBACCO LOTTERY
Signed by Daniel of St. Thos. Jenifer.
Original in Kremer Collection.

a Proclamation announcing a day to be devoted to "Fasting, Humiliation and Prayer." The date was chosen for a Thursday, perhaps in memory of the custom of Thanksgiving in the Plymouth Colony.

A Proclamation

The Goodness of the Supreme Being to all his rational Creatures, demands their acknowledgments of gratitude and Love. His absolute Government of the World dictates that it is the Interest of every Nation and People ardently to supplicate his favour and implore his Protection.

When the Lust of Dominion, or lawless Ambition excites Arbitrary Power to invade the Rights, or endeavour to wrest from a People their Sacred and invaluable Privileges, and compels them, in Defence of the same; to encounter all the Horrors and Calamities of a bloody and vindictive War, then is that People loudly called upon to fly unto that God, for Protection, who hears the Cries of the Distressed, and will not turn a deaf Ear to the Supplication of the oppressed.

Great Britain, hitherto left to infatuated Counsels, and to pursue measures repugnant to her own Interest, and distressing to this Country; still persists in the design of Subjugating these United

States which will Compel us into another active, and perhaps bloody Campaign.

The United States in Congress assembled, therefore taking into consideration our present Situation, our multiplied Transgressions of the holy Laws of our God, and his past acts of Kindness and Goodness toward us which we ought to record with the liveliest Gratitude; think it their indispensable Duty to call upon the Several States to set apart the last Thursday in April next as a Day of Fasting, Humiliation and Prayer; that our Joint Supplications may then ascend to the Throne of the Ruler of the Universe, Beseeching him to diffuse a Spirit of Universal Reformation among all Ranks and Degrees of our Citizens, and make us a holy that so we may be an happy People; that it would please him to impart Wisdom, Integrity, and Unanimity to our Counsellors, to bless and prosper the reign of our illustrious Ally, and give success to his Arms employed in the defence of the rights of human nature; that he would smile upon our military arrangements by land and sea, administer comfort and Consolation to our prisoners in a Cruel Captivity, protect the health and life of our Commander in Chief, grant us victory over our Enemies, establish peace in all our Borders, and give happiness to all our

Inhabitants; That he would prosper the labour of the husbandman, making the earth yield its increase in abundance and give a proper season for the ingathering of the Fruits thereof; That he would grant success to all engaged in lawful trade and Commerce and take under his Guardianship all Schools and Seminaries of learning and make them nurseries of virtue and piety; that he would incline the hearts of all men to peace and fill them with Universal Charity, and benevolence and that the religion of our divine Redeemer with all its benign influences may cover the earth as the Waters cover the sea.

> Done by the United States in Congress Assembled this nineteenth day of March in the Year of our Lord one thousand Seven hundred and eighty two and in the Sixth Year of our Indepence.
>
> JOHN HANSON, Presd.

Attest:

Chas Thompson, Secy.

John Hanson was now sixty-six years of age, and for the past eight years had been carrying a load of duty and responsibility more fitted for a younger man. Who can know the miles that he had travelled on horse back, the discomforts which he had experienced without giving them a thought. He was seventeen years older than Washington, and had few seniors among the great men of the Revolution, one of these being the phenomenal and perennial Franklin. Now at the climax of his career the strain became too great. In mid-April, 1782, the Congress assembled without his presence, and Daniel Carroll, his associate from Maryland, was named to preside over the sessions in the absence of the President. Hanson continued to sign all official papers, and performed most of his duties until the conclusion of his term.

He took a lively interest in the organization of the Post Office Department, and it made great progress during the period of his presidency. Even a brief review of the official correspondence of the President in 1782 indicates how remarkably well the young government was able to function, despite numerous clumsy forms and customs and many indirections of authority. Time and again the Congress felt called upon, not to pass laws, but to recommend that each state should pass certain laws. Nevertheless things were done. The remnants of British resistance in the field were being stamped out. Robert Morris was getting a banking system under way. Franklin and others were establishing our foreign contacts more firmly. Washington was tirelessly cleaning up the final details of his commandership of the armed forces. He wrote frequently to Hanson, seeking and giving advice and information.

That Hanson was fulfilling whatever understanding he may have had with Washington for giving to the General the greater confidence of the Congress, is well evidenced by the authority forwarded under Hanson's signature on September 16, 1782, dealing with the exchange of prisoners of war. It is noteworthy that the Congress appointed no Committee for this purpose, drew up no formulas or rules, but left all to the sound judgment of the commander in the field. It was—

"Resolved, That the following commission be executed and transmitted to His Excellency General Washington.

THE UNITED STATES IN CONGRESS ASSEMBLED TO ALL PEOPLE WHO SHALL SEE THESE PRESENTS, SEND GREETING:

Whereas, Justice and humanity and the practice of civilized nations, require that the calamities and asperities of war should as far as possible be mitigated; and we being disposed for that benevolent purpose to accede to a general cartel between the United States of America and the British nation, for the exchange, subsistence and better treatment of all prisoners of war. Now therefore, KNOW YE, that reposing high confidence in the wisdom, prudence and integrity of our truly and well beloved George Washington, Esquire, our Commander-in-Chief of all our armies, raised or to be raised for the defense of the United States of America, we have authorized and empowered, and by these presents do authorize and empower our said Commander-in-Chief for us and in our name to negotiate, accede to and establish, in the proper forms and with the usual solemnities, such general cartel between the United States in Congress assembled and the King of Great Britain, for the exchange, subsistence, and better treatment of all prisoners of war, as well land as naval prisoners, hereby giving and granting to our said Commander-in-Chief full power and authority, ultimately and on all points, to adjust, and conclude the principles, terms and conditions of the said cartel, and in general to do and perform every matter and thing which shall in any wise be necessary for the final and perfect accomplishment thereof.

And the better to enable our said Commander-in-Chief to execute the trust reposed in him by these presents, we do hereby further authorize and empower him, from time to time, by commission under his hand, and seal, to nominate and constitute such and so many commissioners as he shall judge necessary, to meet, treat, confer and agree with commissioners to be appointed and competently authorized on the part of the King of Great Britain, touching the terms, conditions and stipulations for subsisting, better treating and exchanging all prisoners of war, as aforesaid, as well as for liquidating and settling all accounts and claims whatsoever, respecting the maintenance and subsisting of prisoners of war on either side; and we do hereby declare that the engagements concluded upon by our said Commander-in-Chief in the premises, being mutually interchanged with the party contracting on behalf of the Crown and nation of Great Britain, shall be binding and conclusive on the United States of America.

IN TESTIMONY WHEROF, We have caused these, our letters, to be made patent, and the great seal of the United States of America to be thereunto affixed:

Witness, His Excellency, John Hanson, Esquire, President of the United States in Congress Assembled, the sixteenth day of September, in the year of our Lord, one thousand seven hundred and eighty-two, and of our sovereignty and independence the seventh.

(Signed)   JOHN HANSON, President.

The correspondence with Dr. Thomas evidently continued through the year, although much of it may not have been preserved. Late in October Hanson wrote to his son-in-law with satisfaction because Holland had recognized the Independence of the United States. A little later there went forward the last known letter of the series.

Philadelphia,
Oct. 2d, 1782

DEAR DOCTOR:
My presidentship expires the first Monday in next month, and we can't set out for some days after. * * * Our European intelligence respecting the negotiations for peace is not very favor-

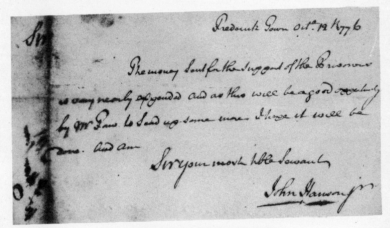

**LETTER TO JOHN HANSON
FROM DANIEL OF ST. THOS. JENIFER**
Original in **Kremer** Collection.

able. It appears the British minister is for procrastination, in hopes it may be supposed of another 12th of April, they will be for trying the fortunes of another campaign and trust to the chapter of accidents. Congress has just received late advices from Canada; between 3,000 and 4,000 British troops are expected there from England, and 1,500 foreign troops from New York, to strengthen their position in that Country, while the whole force of the British nation is to be employed against the French and Spanish possessions in the West Indies. Colonel Campbell, agent for Indian affairs, has had a meeting with the Indians (at which our informant was present). He told them that the King had ordered him to acquaint them that, from COMPASSION TO HIS AMERICAN SUBJECTS, he had ordered that all hostilities against them should cease; that, therefore, they must not in future make any incursions or commit any ravages upon them until further orders. The Indian Sachem answered that he was very sensible of the present situation of the Indians, and of the English; that the Americans had beat them everywhere, and that the English was no longer able to carry on the war, that it was time the Indian should look to their own concerns or be sacrificed. He concluded by telling Campbell that he should no longer listen to his lies, and went off much dissatisfied. Transports are gone from New York to take off the garrison at Charles Town. It is probable that this account is true, as preparations for the evacuation of that place have been making for some time. By letters, this day received from General Greene, we have the disagreeable account of the death of that worthy young man and brave officer, Colonel Laurens. He was killed in a skirmish with the enemy near Charles Town with a few others.

Farewell,

JOHN HANSON.

On November 4th, 1782, the new Congress began, and Elias Boudinot was elected President. Upon the retirement of John Hanson, the following resolution, proposed by Mr. Duane, and seconded by Mr. Izard was adopted:

"Resolved, That the thanks of Congress be given to the Hon. John Hanson, late President of Congress, in testimony of their approbation of his conduct in the chair, and in the execution of public business."

The conclusion of his Presidency found Hanson borne down sorely by ill health and the weight

170

of years. During the summer of 1783 he rallied somewhat, was about among his family and affairs in Maryland, cheerful but only active within narrow limits. In the autumn he went to visit a nephew, Thomas Hanson, at Oxon Hill. There his last illness came upon him, and on November 22, 1783, he died. It seems probable that he was buried on his nephew's estate, as would have been the custom. If so even the exact location of his grave is lost to time.

Chapter VIII

THE SCANDINAVIAN INFLUENCE
IN AMERICA

$\mathcal{M}$ORE THAN A CENTURY
would pass after John Hanson was laid at rest in
Maryland before the nation he had helped to
build would move to do him honor. Thirty-two
new states would have been added to the original
thirteen before his statue would be dedicated in
the nation's Capitol, placed there by Maryland
beside the statue of Charles Carroll in January,
1903. The foresight of John Hanson and his col-
leagues in the Maryland assembly and the Continental Congress, insisting that the western lands
be made the property of the whole nation and
subsequently created into new, separate and sovereign states, made possible the addition of those
states.

The influence of the great man of Charles and
Frederick Counties therefore went on through
years and decades. Nor was Maryland for many
generations without the services of men descended

175

from the four Hanson brothers who had come to America as wards of Queen Christina.

John Hanson had married Jane Contee, daughter of Alexander Contee of Prince Georges County and member of a family of distinction in its own right. Alexander Contee was descended from French Huguenots who had fled to England to avoid religious persecution in an earlier century. Alexander had come to America from his family home at Barnstable, accompanying his uncle John Contee to the new world. The children of both John and Alexander Contee were figures of importance in the history of their state.

John Hanson and Jane Contee Hanson were the parents of eight children, three of whom died in infancy. Of three surviving sons, two were to perish in their country's uniform. Peter Hanson, a lieutenant of the Maryland Line, fell mortally wounded at Fort Washington in 1776. Samuel, a surgeon with George Washington's Life Guards, died in 1781 from illness incurred in service on the field of battle. This second sacrifice was fresh upon the father's heart when he was elected President of the Congress. It is not to be wondered that he should have written to his son-in-law that family matters called him homeward, and only the absolute requirements of duty kept him in

JOHN HANSON
Statue in Statuary Hall, United States Capitol.

Philadelphia to serve the cause for which two sons had fallen.

Alexander Contee Hanson, the oldest son, was a man of mature years at the beginning of the Revolution, a judge in Frederick County. He remained in judicial service of the state throughout his life. During the war it fell to his lot to preside at the trial of seven Tories, charged with plotting an escape of British prisoners of war who were confined in Frederick. He was one of the last judges in America ever to pronounce the fearful sentence for the traitor which had come down through the Middle Ages, "to be hanged, drawn, and quartered." That dreadful punishment was duly executed upon three ring leaders of the Frederick plot.

Jane Contee Hanson, named after her mother, became the wife of Dr. Philip Thomas and the mother of a distinguished family. It was to Philip Thomas that John Hanson wrote the few letters of a personal nature which have been preserved from the period of his Presidency of the Congress. The letters which are of record do not relate another tragedy in the old age of President Hanson —Jane Thomas was on her death bed when he went to Congress in 1781. Catherine Contee Hanson, a younger daughter, married Philip Alexander.

All of the Hanson children were survived by their mother, who lived in Frederick until 1812, a gracious old lady of 85 surrounded, happily, by grandchildren and beloved by her neighbors. One of her grandchildren, son and namesake of Alexander Contee Hanson, was then a figure of the stirring struggles of the Federalists and the Republicans. Belonging to the old conservative party, he had served in Congress and was editor of a Federalist newspaper in Baltimore. His printing plant suffered an attack by an infuriated mob, while Federalist leaders rushed to his assistance. What amounted almost to a battle was fought around the building, old General Lingan, a Revolutionary hero, losing his life at the hands of the mob, while Light Horse Harry Lee, the Virginia soldier, was wounded, and Hanson badly beaten. He fled to his grandfather's old neighborhood in Charles County, and the mob was quelled by militia. Within a few years Alexander Contee Hanson had been returned to the Senate from Maryland, and later achieved considerable fame by the fighting of a duel. He remained a potent figure in public life for many years.

The whole of Maryland history is filled with

records of the Hanson connections. Daniel of St. Thomas Jenifer, a nephew of John Hanson, was a member of the Constitutional Convention. The Jenifers and the Stones and the Briscoes and other kin produced soldiers and statesmen who attained fame in national affairs.

In much the same manner that the John Hanson family spread through southern Maryland, the branch of the family headed by the first Andrew Hanson achieved distinction in the counties on the Eastern Shore. Andrew's son Hans Hanson, of Kimbolton, married Martha Kelto Ward. They had a grandson, Gustavus Hanson, serving on Committees of Observation and the like in revolutionary times, meeting his cousin John Hanson in the deliberations at Annapolis. A comprehensive record of many branches of the Hanson family had been perpetuated by George A. Hanson, a great grandson of Gustavus, in his book "Kent Island—The Eastern Shore."

No other Scandinavian family which moved into Maryland from New Sweden achieved the note attaching to the Hansons, although several distinguished sons of Sweden became famous in the Free State. Early in the 18th century Gustav Hesselius, portrait painter from the Swedish court, moved from Philadelphia to Prince Georges County, Maryland. He was followed by his son, John Hesselius, probably the first painter of permanent and world wide note produced by the New World. The younger artist painted many of the leading figures of his day, including the distinguished John Hanson of Mulberry Grove. He was a teacher of Charles Willson Peale, painter extraordinary of Revolutionary days, whose subjects likewise included John Hanson and also George Washington and many other leading men. Peale was the father of the artist, Rembrandt Peale.

While New Sweden gave substantially of her pioneer blood to the neighboring lands of Maryland, a great number of the Swedish and Finnish families remained along the Delaware, while others crossed into New Jersey and on to settlements on the distant Hudson, or North River. The mother of James Fenimore Cooper was of one such family, a Swede who traced her ancestry to Tinicum Island where Johan Printz had made his capital.

Pennsylvania for many years has honored her John Morton, signer of the Declaration of Independence, direct descendant of an immigrant from Sweden to the Delaware. The leading Swedish American historian of the present day, Dr. Amandus Johnson, presides over the John Morton Memorial Museum at Philadelphia. To the tireless research of Dr. Johnson both in this country and in the libraries of Stockholm we owe much of what has been preserved and published of the records of New Sweden, dating back to the first conceptions of a Swedish trading company in the New World fostered in the mind of Gustavus Adolphus.

Into the life of Pennsylvania, Delaware, Maryland and New Jersey the strain of Scandinavian blood from the first Swedish and Finnish colonists was gradually absorbed. For years after the Dutch and then the English had taken possession of New Sweden and severed governmental ties with the old homelands, the Swedish and Finnish churches continued to send out pastors to America to minister to the Lutheran parishes which retained their entity and their languages along the Delaware. Through church and school something of the Scandinavian culture remained in revolutionary times. The rosters of the Continental Army abound in Swedish names. The same is true of every army ever mustered beneath the Stars and Stripes. The hardy men and women of the Kalmar Nyckel and the Fogel Grip have left an indelible impress upon the bulwarks of our civilization. Three hundred years ago, they fostered a liberty of thought and a democracy of social order. From their first clearings on the wild shores of a new land there has gone out a spirit of pioneering conquest by men of individual character and courage that has spread across the face of the whole continent as surely and as steadily as the broad Delaware flows tireless to the sea.

BIBLIOGRAPHY

ACKNOWLEDGMENTS AND SOURCES

$\mathcal{O}$CCASIONAL REFERENCE
has been made in the text of the sources most frequently consulted, and a short bibliography is ap-
pended. In addition the inspiration and effort
involved in preparing this book have had numerous happy contributions from friends and ac-
quaintances and contacts directly and indirectly
established.

The C. W. Peale portrait of John Hanson hangs
in Independence Hall at Philadelphia, whose
Curator, Mr. Horace Thompson Carpenter,
granted permission for its reproduction.

The Hesselius portraits are the property of
Alice Lee Thomas Stevenson (Mrs. Robert H.
Stevenson) of Boston, the daughter of Douglas H.
Thomas of Baltimore whose book on John Han-
son is elsewhere referred to, and the copies for use
herein were furnished, with permission of Mrs.
Stevenson, by the Frick Library of Art of New

York City. Mrs. Stevenson also has most of the few John Hanson letters known to exist. Through John Hanson's daughter, Jane Contee Hanson, who married Philip Thomas, Mrs. Stevenson bears direct descent from the Maryland patriot.

To Emil Hurja my thanks for the use of his comprehensive collection of historical manuscripts.

Extensive use has been made of the facilities of the Library of Congress and valued assistance given by Dr. Thomas P. Martin, of its manuscript division, and Mr. George H. Milne. The same is true of the Pennsylvania Historical Society, and of the Maryland Historical society and its Director, Dr. J. H. Pleasants, and Florence J. Kennedy, its Librarian.

Acknowledgment is made of my thanks to Richard Seelye Jones, of Washington, for research and editorial assistance.

Mr. Swepson Earle, who has written much of value concerning his state of Maryland, and William N. Morrell, Esq., of Washington, a student of Scandinavian participation in American history, contributed valued suggestions.

The following works cover many phases of the

ancestry, historical background, life and times of
John Hanson of Mulberry Grove:

ACRELIUS, ISRAEL, *A History of New Sweden.* Philadelphia, 1874.

ANDREWS, CHARLES MCLEAN, *The Fathers of New
England.* New Haven, 1919.

ANDREWS, MATTHEW PAGE, *The Founding of Maryland.* New York, 1933.

Archives of Maryland, Maryland Historical Society,
Baltimore, 1883-1919.

BANCROFT, GEORGE, *History of the United States of
America.* New York, 1891.

CAMPANIUS HOLM, TOMAS, *Description of the
Province of New Sweden.* Stockholm, 1702.

CLAY, JEHU CURTIS, *Annals of the Swedes on the Delaware.* Chicago, 1938.

Documents, Compiled from Manuscripts at Albany,
and in the Royal Archives at Stockholm. Albany,
1877.

DODGE, THEODORE AYRAULT, *Gustavus Adolphus.*
Boston, 1895.

EARLE, SWEPSON, *The Chesapeake Bay Country.*

FERRIS, BENJAMIN, *A History of the Original Settlements on the Delaware.* Wilmington, 1846.

GLENN, THOMAS ALLEN, *Some Colonial Mansions
and Those Who Lived in Them.* Philadelphia,
1900.

HANSON, GEORGE ADOLPHUS, *Old Kent—The Eastern
Shore of Maryland.* Baltimore, 1876.

HART, ALBERT BUSHNELL, *Swedish Americanism.* Philadelphia, 1929.

JOHNSON, AMANDUS, *The Swedes in America.* Philadelphia, 1914.

JOHNSON, AMANDUS, *The Swedish Settlements on the Delaware.* Philadelphia, 1911.

LOUHI, EVERT ALEXANDER, *The Delaware Finns.* New York, 1925.

New York Historical Records—Vol. XII. Albany, 1877.

RICHARDSON, MRS. HESTER DORSEY, *Side-Lights on Maryland History.* Baltimore, 1913.

SCARBOROUGH, KATHERINE, *Homes of the Cavaliers.* New York, 1930.

SMITH, SEYMOUR WEMYSS, *John Hanson, Our First President.* New York, 1932.

The Swedish Element in America, Swedish-American Biographical Society, Chicago, 1931.

Tercentenary History of Maryland. Baltimore, 1925.

THOMAS, DOUGLAS H., *John Hanson, President of the United States in Congress Assembled.* Baltimore, 1898.

WARD, CHRISTOPHER, *The Dutch and Swedes on the Delaware.* Philadelphia, 1930.

WILLIAMS, THOMAS JOHN CHEW, *History of Frederick County, Maryland.* Frederick, Md., 1910.

WILSTACH, PAUL, *Potomac Landings.*

WINSOR, JUSTIN, *Narrative and Critical History of America.* New York, 1884.

WUORINEN, JOHN H., *The Finns on the Delaware.* New York, 1938.